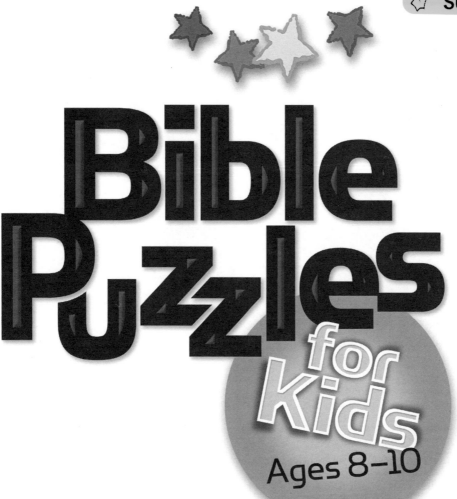

Bible Puzzles

for Kids

Ages 8–10

With puzzles created by

Ellen Humbert

Sheryl J. Johnson

Elaina Meyers

William Schlegl

John Hudson Tiner

Standard
PUBLISHING

Cincinnati, Ohio

Bible Puzzles for Kids Ages 8–10

This book is a revision of *Bible Puzzles for Kids Ages 8–12*, © 2000.

All Scripture quotations, unless otherwise indicated, are taken from the *HOLY BIBLE, NEW INTERNATIONAL VERSION*®. *NIV*®. Copyright 1973, 1978, 1984 by Biblica, Inc.™ Used by permission of Zondervan. All rights reserved.

Credits
Puzzles written by Ellen Humbert, Sheryl J. Johnson, Elaina Meyers, William Schlegl, John Hudson Tiner
Cover design by Liz Malwitz
Interior design by Scott Ryan
Illustrated by Mike McKee
Project editors: Christine Spence, Ruth Frederick, Chris Wallace

Published by Standard Publishing, Cincinnati, Ohio.
www.standardpub.com

15 14 13 12 11 10   6 7 8 9 10 11 12 13 14

ISBN-13: 978-0-7847-1788-2
ISBN-10: 0-7847-1788-5

Contents

Table of Contents

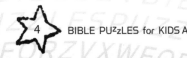

Table of Contents

Table of Contents

Bible Memory Puzzles

Introduction

This book contains 124 Bible puzzles that help you teach important Bible facts. Each puzzle
- contains a Scripture reference and a Bible-story topic for easy reference (Bible Memory puzzles include only a reference),
- is able to be photocopied, for use many times with many different students,
- is a complete activity, with no extra materials (other than a pencil) required (exceptions include page 26, which requires a calculator for figuring square roots, and page 62, which requires a mirror),
- reinforces and teaches Bible facts,
- correlates with a Scripture from Standard Publishing's HeartShaper® Middle Elementary curriculum, and
- contains a separate answer key on pages 134–140.

How to Find the Puzzles You Want

To find a puzzle based on a particular Scripture, look in the table of contents on pages 3–6. The first 103 puzzles are based on Bible stories or Bible passages and are arranged in order through the Bible, beginning with Genesis and ending with Revelation. The last 21 puzzles are based on Bible Memory verses and are also arranged in order through the Bible.

To find a puzzle that correlates with a particular lesson in Standard Publishing's HeartShaper® Middle Elementary Sunday school curriculum, look at the Scope & Sequence on pages 141–143 of this book. Find the quarter and lesson that you are teaching, and you will be directed to the page in this book that contains the correlating puzzle. (Not every Bible Memory verse will have a correlated puzzle.)

Creative Counting

Look at the story of creation in the first chapter of Genesis. Use information from the story to complete this puzzle.

ACROSS

1. On which day did God create man and woman?

4. On which day did God create fish and fowl?

5. What did God do on the seventh day?

7. On which day did God create the sun and moon?

DOWN

2. On which day did God create trees and grass?

3. On which day did God create day and night?

6. On which day did God create the sky?

The Fall
—Genesis 2, 3

Gardener's Dilemma

In the beginning, the Garden of Eden was the perfect place for the man and woman who lived there. But something went terribly wrong, and they couldn't stay. Read Genesis 2 and 3. Then put on your gardening hat and identify some of the "growing things" mentioned in this Bible story.

Unscramble the letters in each section of the garden and write your answer on its line.

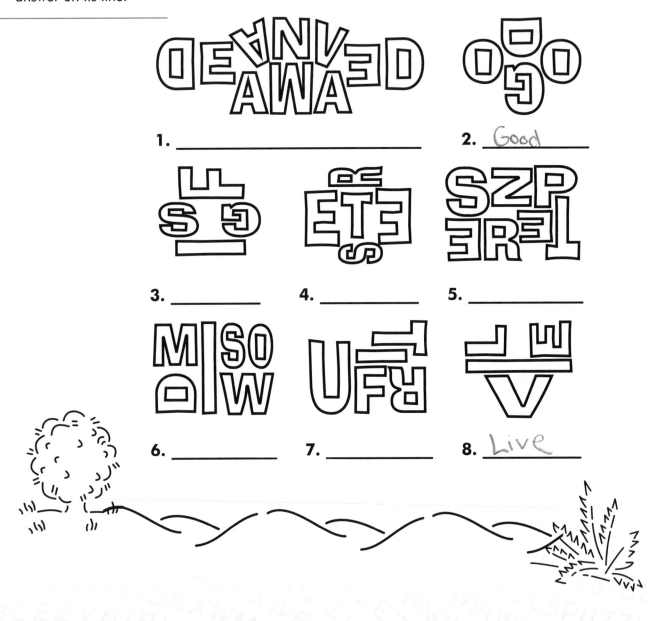

1. _____   2. _Good_____

3. _____   4. _____   5. _____

6. _____   7. _____   8. _Live_____

What Did Noah Find?

To unwind this puzzle, start at the arrow. Moving clockwise, write down every other letter from the circle's edge on the answer line. Cross out the letters on the circle as you use them. You will read around the circle twice to complete your answer.

Noah found all the stuff
To build a great big boat.
And Noah found the courage
To believe the boat would
   float!

But what else
did Noah find?

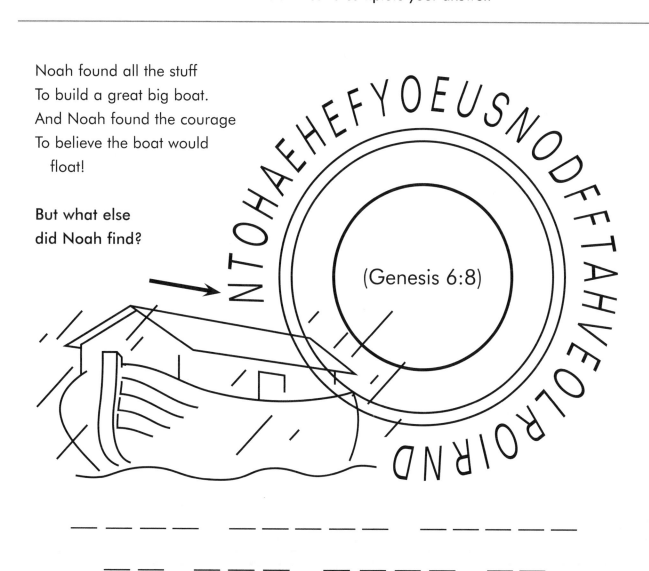

(Genesis 6:8)

__ ___ _____ ___ ____

__ ___ _____ ____

___ _____ .

A Very Special Project

When people become so interested in a very special project that they forget about God, confusion may be the result! That's what happened in Genesis 11:1-9. Read the Scripture and fill in the clues. (A=Across, D=Down)

CLUES

1. This story takes place in the country of (1-D), another name for Shinar.

2. The people settled on a (2-A) in (5-A).

3. They built their city from (5-D) instead of (4-A).

4. They planned to build a very tall (4-D).

5. It would reach to the (2-D).

6. The people wanted to make a (3-D) for themselves.

7. But the (6-A) confused their (1-A).

8. Did the people ever finish their very special project? (3-A).

Moving Day

God led Abram to a new land—a land of milk and honey. Can you help Abram find his way through this maze? Use verses from Genesis 12 as a road map to follow.

1 He started his journey from Genesis 12:5.

2 He traveled through Canaan to a great tree of Moreh at Genesis 12:6.

3 He went further and camped in the hills between Genesis 12:8.

4 Then he traveled to the desert lands of Genesis 12:9.

5 He dreamed of the day he would pitch his tent in the new land God promised.

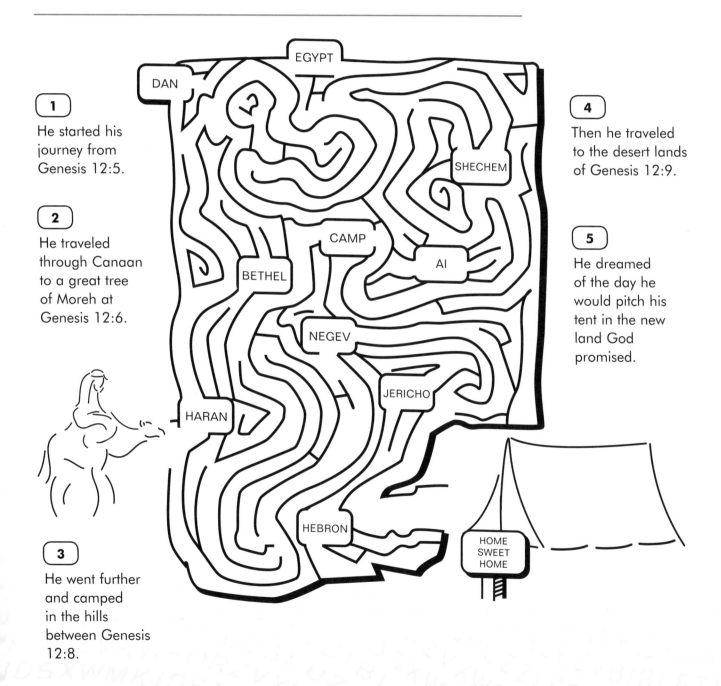

Birth of Isaac
—Genesis 17, 18, 21

What's in a Name?

Names are important. It **h**as been so from the beginning.

Among the tribes of Old **T**estament times, it was a common custom to include a name for God as part of a chi**l**d's name. For instance, Oba**d**iah means "servant of Jehovah." Special events occ**u**rring before, during, or after the chi**l**d's birth might also be reflected in the chosen nam**e**.

Girls were o**f**ten named for beautiful objects in natu**r**e, or pleasant qualities of character. For instance, **S**alome means "peace."

(8) (5) (1) (11) (6) (2) (12) (7) (3) (4) (9) (10)

1. Isaac

☐☐ ☐☐☐G☐☐
5 3 7 1 12 5 10

2. Moses

☐☐☐W☐
2 9 1 8

O☐☐
12 11

3. Adam

M☐☐
1 8

4. Sarah

P☐☐☐C☐☐☐
9 6 8 3 10 10

5. Eve

☐☐☐☐
7 6 4 3

Use the numbered letters from the box above to fill in the empty squares. Discover the meanings of these famous names.

Your Answer

After reading the text that follows, arrange the underlined letters to fill in the blanks beside Abraham's picture.

God asked Abraham to do a very difficult thing in sacrificing his son, Isaac. But Abraham trusted God and set out for the region of Moriah. His faith was strong, and he tried to be obedient in all things. Every day he listened for God's voice in his life. When God calls your name, will you be listening?

Will you be ready to follow? Just like Abraham, you can say:

What Is It?

Directions: Make a code key by numbering the letters of the alphabet in sequence from 1–26. Let A = 1 and Z = 26. Then use the code key to translate the message.

Esau traded his birthright to Jacob for food. By decoding the following sequence of numbers, you will discover what a birthright meant in Old Testament times.

___ ___ ___ ___ ___ ___ ___ ___ ___ ___ :
2 9 18 20 8 18 9 7 8 20

___   ___ ___ ___ ___ ___   ___ ___ ___ ___ ___
1   4 15 21 2 12 5   19 8 1 18 5

___ ___   ___ ___ ___   ___ ___ ___ ___ ___ ___ ___ ___ ___ ___
15 6   20 8 5   9 14 8 5 18 9 20 1 14 3 5

___ ___ ___   ___ ___ ___ ___ ___ ___ ___ ___ ___ ___
1 14 4   12 5 1 4 5 18 19 8 9 16

___ ___   ___ ___ ___   ___ ___ ___ ___ .
15 6   20 8 5   3 12 1 14

All in the Family

Spell the names of Joseph and his 11 brothers by crossing out the letters you use in the big box below. When you finish, rearrange the letters that are *not* crossed out to discover the name of Joseph's only sister.

```
              E R E A U
          A N E D U A N
      E D A N S       U A N A N
    A D E H N         U P I B I L
  H S N V O           M D C H E I
    A R I H I         B L H R J
      S A T E J       J A G N S
          S L P O M E I
            B Z H
```

Joseph's brothers

Reuben
Simeon
Levi
Judah
Dan
Naphtali
Gad
Asher
Issachar
Zebulun
Joseph
Benjamin

Joseph's only sister was ___ ___ ___ ___ ___.

Computer Glitch

Figure out which letter key is broken in each of the computer screens below. Cross out the Xs and write in the correct letters on each screen. Then number the screens to put the story parts in order.

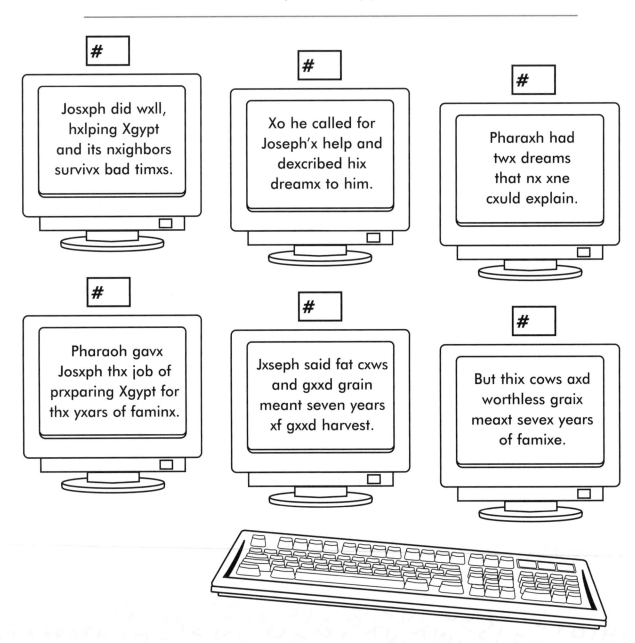

#

Josxph did wxll,
hxlping Xgypt
and its nxighbors
survivx bad timxs.

#

Xo he called for
Joseph'x help and
dexcribed hix
dreamx to him.

#

Pharaxh had
twx dreams
that nx xne
cxuld explain.

#

Pharaoh gavx
Josxph thx job of
prxparing Xgypt for
thx yxars of faminx.

#

Jxseph said fat cxws
and gxxd grain
meant seven years
xf gxxd harvest.

#

But thix cows axd
worthless graix
meaxt sevex years
of famixe.

Adding It Up

Joseph did a great job preparing Egypt for the famine. Even his own brothers traveled from their homeland to buy grain in Egypt. The numbers in this puzzle add up to a special lesson Joseph's whole family learned during a time of need.

Joseph's Jingle

1. _____ far away

2. _____ to live one day.

3. _____ There he did grow.

4. _____ all to know

5. _____ is the key

6. _____ and harmony!

Work out each math problem, writing the answers in the boxes.
Then use the final answers to put the lines of Joseph's Jingle in order.

A. $4 + 3 + 2 + 1 =$ ___ $- 7 =$ ☐ There he did learn.

B. $5 \times 5 =$ ___ $- 19 =$ ☐ to peace and love

C. $12 \times 2 =$ ___ $\div 6 =$ ___ $- 3 =$ ☐ Down in Egypt,

D. $4 + 4 + 4 =$ ___ $- 8 =$ ☐ And now he wants us

E. $6 \times 3 =$ ___ $\div 2 =$ ___ $- 7 =$ ☐ Joseph went

F. $12 - 5 =$ ___ $\times 2 =$ ___ $- 9 =$ ☐ forgiving others

Moses' Birth
—Exodus 2–4

Rescued from the Nile

The squares below are part of a puzzle illustrating God's plan in action, as Pharaoh's daughter discovers Moses and resolves to raise him as her own child. God was making sure Moses would be protected as he grew up.

Study the nine puzzle parts, mentally arranging them in order to complete the picture. Write the letter of each part in this grid, indicating the position of the piece.

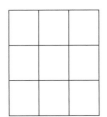

If you wish, the pictures squares can be cut out, arranged so that the sides are touching, and glued to another sheet of paper.

A

B

C

D

E

F

G

H

I

Plaguing Problems

Look for the 10 plagues in this pyramid. They are hidden forwards, backwards, up, down, and diagonally.

When Moses grew up, he was chosen by God to lead the Hebrews out of slavery. God sent plagues to the land of Egypt to help Moses convince Pharaoh to free the people. You can read about it in Exodus 7–14.

PLAGUES

BLOOD
FROGS
GNATS
FLIES
LIVESTOCK
BOILS
HAIL
LOCUST
DARKNESS
DEATH

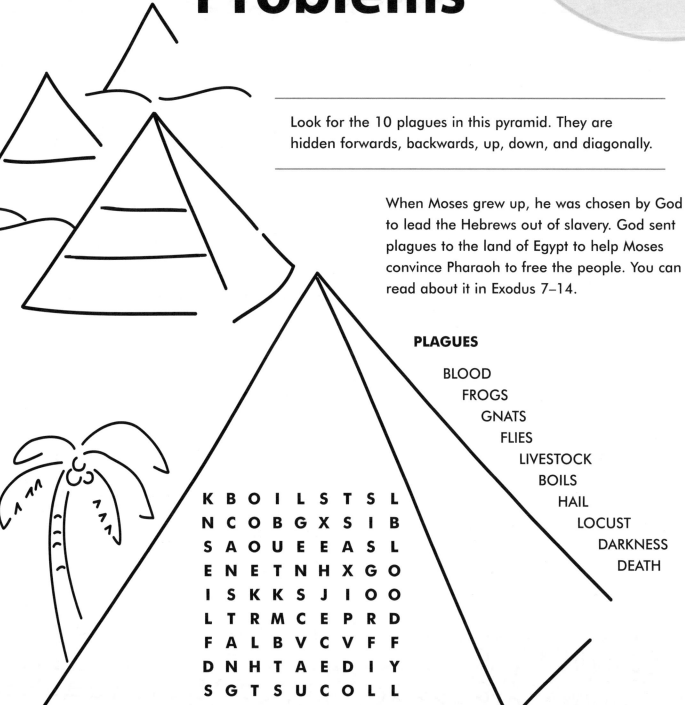

```
K B O I L S T S L
N C O B G X S I B
S A O U E E A S L
E N E T N H X G O
I S K K S J I O O
L T R M C E P R D
F A L B V C V F F
D N H T A E D I Y
S G T S U C O L L
```

Following Directions

God told Moses, and Moses told the people, "Stay in your houses, follow these directions, and you will be safe." In this way, God protected the Israelites from the last and most terrible of the plagues.

God's Directions

Select a <u>1</u> for a special sacrifice.

Mark the door frames of your houses with its <u>2</u>.

Prepare and eat the roasted meat with bitter <u>3</u> and unleavened <u>4</u> for dinner.

Eat quickly, saving <u>5</u> of it for tomorrow.

Wear your <u>6</u> and <u>7</u> during the meal so you can leave quickly.

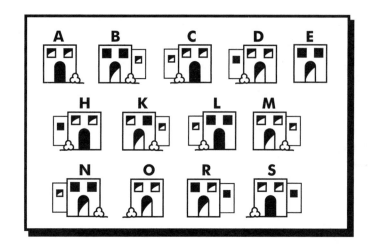

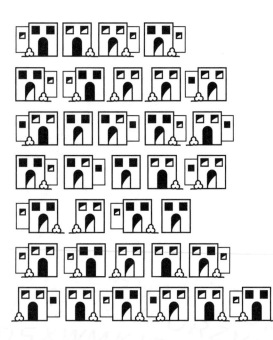

1. _____

2. _____

3. _____

4. _____

5. _____

6. _____

7. _____

Red Sea Fill-in

With Moses as their leader, the Israelites left Egypt.
But Pharaoh sent an army to bring them back!
You can read about it in Exodus 12–14.

The words listed below are from Exodus 12–14.
Fit them into their proper places in the puzzle.
All shared letters have been filled in to give you a head start.

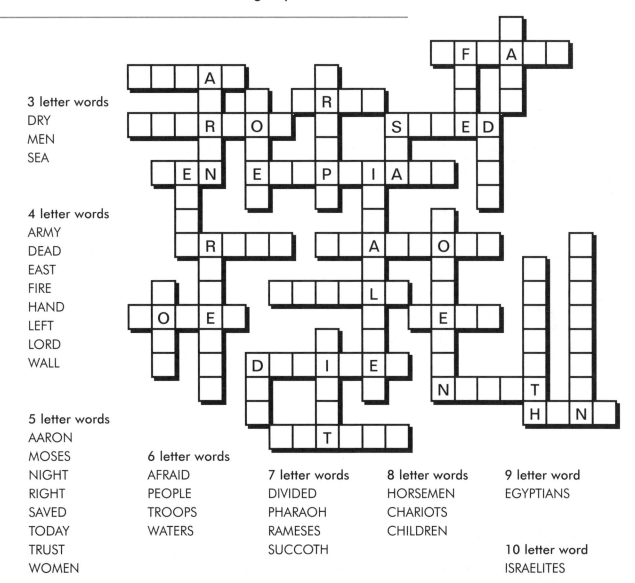

3 letter words
DRY
MEN
SEA

4 letter words
ARMY
DEAD
EAST
FIRE
HAND
LEFT
LORD
WALL

5 letter words
AARON
MOSES
NIGHT
RIGHT
SAVED
TODAY
TRUST
WOMEN

6 letter words
AFRAID
PEOPLE
TROOPS
WATERS

7 letter words
DIVIDED
PHARAOH
RAMESES
SUCCOTH

8 letter words
HORSEMEN
CHARIOTS
CHILDREN

9 letter word
EGYPTIANS

10 letter word
ISRAELITES

Which One?

The Lord appeared to Moses atop Mount Sinai and gave him two tablets of stone. These tablets contained the Ten Commandments. The Ten Commandments are guidelines for leading our lives. Use the diagonal code to discover which commandment Jesus called the most important. (Hint: Start in the upper left-hand corner and read diagonally. The first word is filled in for you.

T	E	S	P	N	N	J	H	E	O	O	D	U
H	O	M	A	A	D	T	H	G	Y	N	O	W
M	I	T	E	E	S	T	R	L	A	Y	D	O
T	R	N	R	I	E	U	L	T	L	N	Y	A
O	O	E	S	V	O	A	R	L	A	L	D	H
T	W	U	O	Y	H	A	A	L	L	N	T	O
S	S	L	D	T	E	H	U	A	I	I	Y	T
E	S	R	I	H	T	O	H	M	W	L	S	N
I	O	W	R	I	S	T	R	D	L	R	E	T
L	D	U	W	R	I	U	N	A	U	R	G	H

"T H E _ _ _ _   _ _ _ _ _ _ _ _   _ _ _,' _ _ _ _ _ _ _ _

_ _ _ _ _ _, "_ _   _ _ _ _ _:...' _ _ _ _   _ _ _   _ _ _ _   _ _ _ _

_ _ _   _ _ _ _   _ _ _   _ _ _ _   _ _ _ _   _ _ _   _ _ _ _

_ _ _ _   _ _ _ _   _ _ _   _ _ _ _   _ _ _   _ _ _ _

_ _ _ _   _ _ _   _ _ _   _ _ _ _ _   _ _ _ _ _ _ _."'

(Mark 12:29, 30)

An Awesome Promise

The children of Israel had wandered in the desert for 40 years. Now they were ready to enter the promised land. Moses had died and Joshua was appointed the new leader of God's chosen people. Follow the words around and around to discover the awesome promise that God gave to Joshua.

```
              N O O N E W I L
  L L T H E D A Y S O F L
  A E S S O I W I L L Y B
  U S E V E R L E A B O E
  O O N O R S A K V E U A
  Y M L F U O Y E E W R B
  T H L R O N U O Y I L L
  S T I W I U O Y H T I E
  N I W S A W I S A E F T
  I A G A P U D N A T S O
```

"__ ___ ____ __ ____ __ ____ __

_____ ___ __ ____ __ __ ___

____. __ _ ___ ____ ____, __ _

____ __ ____ ___; _ ____ ____

_____ ___ ___ _____ ___." (Joshua 1:5)

Crossing the Jordan
—Joshua 3

The Reason

The Lord caused the Red Sea to part and the Jordan River to stop flowing so the Israelites could cross over on dry ground. Use your calculators to find the square root of each number to discover the special reason why God performed such marvelous deeds.

A	B	D	E	F	G	H	I	K	L
121	289	400	100	576	784	169	729	441	225

M	N	O	P	R	S	T	U	W	Y
484	196	841	361	256	529	676	144	625	324

"
—— ——— ———— —— ———— ———
13 10 20 27 20 26 13 27 23 23 29 26 13 11 26 11 15 15

——— ——————— ———— ——— —————
26 13 10 19 10 29 19 15 10 23 29 24 26 13 10 10 11 16 26 13

————— ————— ———— ——— ————
22 27 28 13 26 21 14 29 25 26 13 11 26 26 13 10 13 11 14 20

—— ——— ———— ——— —————————
29 24 26 13 10 15 29 16 20 27 23 19 29 25 10 16 24 12 15

——— —— ———— ——— —————
11 14 20 23 29 26 13 11 26 18 29 12 22 27 28 13 26

—————— ———— ——— ————
11 15 25 11 18 23 24 10 11 16 26 13 10 15 29 16 20

———— ———." (Joshua 4:24)
18 29 12 16 28 29 20

Wall Breaker

A catapult was usually used to help break down the walls around a city. However, the children of Israel had a different kind of wall breaker. Solve the problems to discover the strange way the Israelites broke down the walls of Jericho.

A. $(3 \times 4) + 2 =$ **C.** $(6 \times 8) + 2 =$ **D.** $(4 \times 9) + 7 =$ **E.** $(9 \times 9) + 9 =$

G. $(7 \times 3) + 4 =$ **H.** $(5 \times 6) + 4 =$ **I.** $(8 \times 5) + 7 =$ **K.** $(6 \times 7) + 9 =$

L. $(2 \times 5) + 1 =$ **M.** $(3 \times 9) + 4 =$ **N.** $(8 \times 9) + 3 =$ **O.** $(4 \times 4) + 2 =$

P. $(7 \times 5) + 4 =$ **R.** $(9 \times 9) + 4 =$ **S.** $(2 \times 7) + 7 =$ **T.** $(8 \times 8) + 3 =$

U. $(9 \times 6) + 2 =$ **V.** $(4 \times 2) + 2 =$ **W.** $(7 \times 6) + 3 =$ **Y.** $(4 \times 6) + 5 =$

___ ___ ___ ___   ___ ___ ___   ___ ___ ___ ___ ___ ___ ___ ___   ___ ___ ___ ___ ___ ___ ___,
45 34 90 75   67 34 90   67 85 56 31 39 90 67 21   21 18 56 75 43 90 43

___ ___ ___   ___ ___ ___ ___ ___ ___   ___ ___ ___ ___ ___ ___ ___,. . .___ ___ ___ ___   ___ ___ ___
67 34 90   39 90 18 39 11 90   21 34 18 56 67 90 43   45 34 90 75   67 34 90

___ ___ ___ ___ ___ ___   ___ ___ ___ ___   ___ ___   ___ ___ ___ ___   ___ ___ ___ ___ ___,
39 90 18 39 11 90   25 14 10 90   14   11 18 56 43   21 34 18 56 67

___ ___ ___   ___ ___ ___ ___   ___ ___ ___ ___ ___ ___ ___ ___ ___;   ___ ___   ___ ___ ___ ___ ___
67 34 90   45 14 11 11   50 18 11 11 14 39 21 90 43   21 18   90 10 90 85 29

___ ___ ___   ___ ___ ___ ___ ___ ___ ___   ___ ___ ___ ___ ___ ___ ___ ___ ___   ___ ___,___ ___ ___
31 14 75   50 34 14 85 25 90 43   21 67 85 14 47 25 34 67   47 75   14 75 43

___ ___ ___ ___   ___ ___ ___ ___ ___   ___ ___ ___   ___ ___ ___ ___.   (Joshua 6:20)
67 34 90 29   67 18 18 51   67 34 90   50 47 67 29

A Special Task

Deborah was a prophetess chosen by God to lead and guide the children of Israel. Write the letter that comes between the two letters given to discover the special task Deborah did for the people.

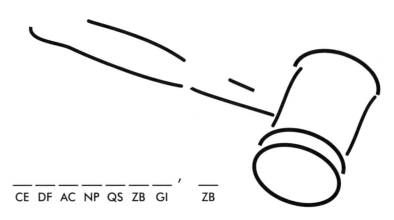

_____ _____ _____ _____ _____ _____ _____   _____ ’
CE   DF   AC   NP   QS   ZB   GI   ZB

_____ _____ _____ _____ _____ _____ _____ _____ _____ ’   _____ _____ _____   _____ _____ _____ _____   _____ _____
OQ   QS   NP   OQ   GI   DF   SU   DF   RT   RT   SU   GI   DF   VX   HJ   EG   DF   NP   EG

_____ _____ _____ _____ _____ _____ _____ _____ _____ ’   _____ _____ _____   _____ _____ _____ _____ _____ _____ _____
KM   ZB   OQ   OQ   HJ   CE   NP   SU   GI   VX   ZB   RT   KM   DF   ZB   CE   HJ   MO   FH

_____ _____ _____ _____ _____ _____   _____ _____   _____ _____ _____ _____   _____ _____ _____ _____ .
HJ   RT   QS   ZB   DF   KM   ZB   SU   SU   GI   ZB   SU   SU   HJ   LN   DF

_____ _____ _____   _____ _____ _____ _____   _____ _____ _____ _____ _____   _____ _____ _____ _____ _____   _____ _____ _____
RT   GI   DF   GI   DF   KM   CE   BD   NP   TV   QS   SU   TV   MO   CE   DF   QS   SU   GI   DF

_____ _____ _____ _____   _____ _____   _____ _____ _____ _____ _____ _____ _____ . . . _____ _____ _____   _____ _____ _____
OQ   ZB   KM   LN   NP   EG   CE   DF   AC   NP   QS   ZB   GI   ZB   MO   CE   SU   GI   DF

_____ _____ _____ _____ _____ _____ _____ _____ _____ _____   _____ _____ _____ _____   _____ _____ _____   _____ _____ _____ _____
HJ   RT   QS   ZB   DF   KM   HJ   SU   DF   RT   BD   ZB   LN   DF   SU   NP   GI   DF   QS   SU   NP

_____ _____ _____ _____   _____ _____ _____ _____ _____   _____ _____ _____ _____ _____ _____ _____ _____   _____ _____ _____ _____ _____ _____ _____ .
GI   ZB   UW   DF   SU   GI   DF   HJ   QS   CE   HJ   RT   OQ   TV   SU   DF   RT   CE   DF   BD   HJ   CE   DF   CE

(Judges 4:4, 5)

Impossible Odds

The Midianites invaded the land of Israel with so many men and camels that is was impossible to count them. Gideon had an army of only 300 men. Use the missing alphabet puzzle to discover how Gideon was able to defeat such a mighty enemy. Find which letter is missing from each line and write it in the spaces below.

```
A B C D E F G H I J K L M N O P Q R S U V W X Y Z
A B C D E F G I J K L M N O P Q R S T U V W X Y Z
A B C D F G H I J K L M N O P Q R S T U V W X Y Z

A B C D E F G H I J K M N O P Q R S T U V W X Y Z
A B C D E F G H I J K L M N P Q R S T U V W X Y Z
A B C D E F G H I J K L M N O P Q S T U V W X Y Z
A B C E F G H I J K L M N O P Q R S T U V W X Y Z

A B D E F G H I J K L M N O P Q R S T U V W X Y Z
A B C D E F G H I J K L M N P Q R S T U V W X Y Z
A B C D E F G H I J K L M O P Q R S T U V W X Y Z
A B C D E G H I J K L M N O P Q R S T U V W X Y Z
A B C D E F G H I J K L M N O P Q R S T V W X Y Z
A B C D E F G H I J K L M N O P Q R T U V W X Y Z
A B C D F G H I J K L M N O P Q R S T U V W X Y Z
A B C E F G H I J K L M N O P Q R S T U V W X Y Z

A B C D E F G H I J K L M N O P Q R S U V W X Y Z
A B C D E F G I J K L M N O P Q R S T U V W X Y Z
A B C D F G H I J K L M N O P Q R S T U V W X Y Z

A B C D F G H I J K L M N O P Q R S T U V W X Y Z
A B C D E F G H I J K L M O P Q R S T U V W X Y Z
A B C D F G H I J K L M N O P Q R S T U V W X Y Z
A B C D E F G H I J K L N O P Q R S T U V W X Y Z
A B C D E F G H I J K L M N O P Q R S T U V W X Z

A B C D E F G H I J K L M N O P Q R T U V W X Y Z
A B C D E F G H I J K L M N P Q R S T U V W X Y Z
A B C D E F G H I J K M N O P Q R S T U V W X Y Z
A B C E F G H I J K L M N O P Q R S T U V W X Y Z
A B C D E F G H J K L M N O P Q R S T U V W X Y Z
A B C D F G H I J K L M N O P Q R S T U V W X Y Z
A B C D E F G H I J K L M N O P Q S T U V W X Y Z
A B C D E F G H I J K L M N O P Q R T U V W X Y Z
```

A Legal Matter

Lawyers today write detailed contracts to complete a legal matter. In Bible times, there was a different way to seal a legal transaction. Write the letter that comes two letters after the letter given to discover this strange legal transaction.

___ ___ ___   ___ ___   ___ ___ ___ ___ ___ ___ ___   ___ ___ ___ ___ ___   ___ ___   ___ ___ ___ ___ ___ ___ '
L M U   G L   C Y P J G C P   R G K C Q   G L   G Q P Y C J

___ ___ ___   ___ ___ ___   ___ ___ ___ ___ ___ ___ ___ ___ ___   ___ ___ ___   ___ ___ ___ ___ ___ ___ ___ ___
D M P   R F C   P C B C K N R G M L   Y L B   R P Y L Q D C P

___ ___   ___ ___ ___ ___ ___ ___ ___   ___ ___   ___ ___ ___ ___ ___   ___ ___ ___ ___ '   ___ ___ ___
M D   N P M N C P R W   R M   Z C A M K C   D G L Y J   M L C

___ ___ ___ ___   ___ ___ ___ ___   ___ ___ ___   ___ ___ ___   ___ ___ ___ ___ ___ ___   ___ ___ ___
N Y P R W   R M M I   M D D   F G Q   Q Y L B Y J   Y L B

___ ___ ___ ___   ___ ___   ___ ___   ___ ___ ___   ___ ___ ___ ___ ___ .   ___ ___ ___ ___   ___ ___ ___
E Y T C   G R   R M   R F C   M R F C P   R F G Q   U Y Q

___ ___ ___   ___ ___ ___ ___ ___ ___   ___ ___   ___ ___ ___ ___ ___ ___ ___ ___ ___ ___
R F C   K C R F M B   M D   J C E Y J G X G L E

___ ___ ___ ___ ___ ___ ___ ___ ___ ___ ___   ___ ___   ___ ___ ___ ___ ___ ___ .
R P Y L Q Y A R G M L Q   G L   G Q P Y C J

(Ruth 4:7)

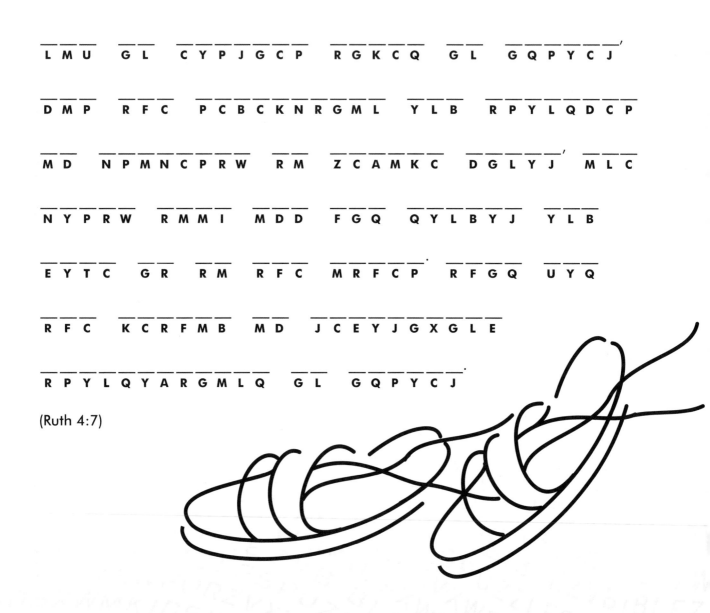

Who Did It?

The children of Israel wanted a king to lead them. Samuel the prophet had the task of presenting the king to the Israelites. But who was it that actually anointed Saul the first king of Israel?

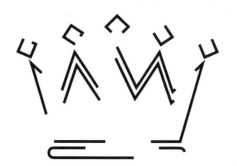

Add the numbers in the box to complete the code and finish the puzzle.

___ ___ ___ ___   ___ ___ ___ ___ ___ ___   ___ ___ ___ ___
12 14 27 24   29 16 26 22 27 15   12 13 13 11

___   ___ ___ ___ ___ ___   ___ ___   ___ ___ ___   ___ ___ ___
16   10 15 16 29 11   13 10   13 28 15   16 24 25

___ ___ ___ ___ ___ ___   ___ ___   ___ ___   ___ ___ ___ ___ ___ ___ ' ___
18 13 22 20 27 25   28 12   13 24   29 16 22 15 29

___ ___ ___ ___   ___ ___ ___   ___ ___ ___ ___ ___ ___   ___ ___ ___ '
14 27 16 25   16 24 25   11 28 29 29 27 25   14 28 26

___ ___ ___ ___ ___ ___ ' " ___ ___ ___   ___ ___ ___   ___ ___ ___
29 16 21 28 24 23   14 16 29   24 13 12   12 14 27

___ ___ ___ ___   ___ ___ ___ ___ ___ ___ ___ ___   ___ ___ ___
15 13 20 25   16 24 13 28 24 12 27 25   21 13 22

___ ___ ___ ___ ___ ___   ___ ___ ___ ___   ___ ___ ___
15 27 16 25 27 20   13 17 27 20   14 28 29

___ ___ ___ ___ ___ ___ ___ ___ ___ ___ ___ ?" (1 Samuel 10:1)
28 24 14 27 20 28 12 16 24 19 27

A	$2 + 3 + 5 + 6$ =	___
C	$4 + 3 + 7 + 5$ =	___
D	$6 + 4 + 7 + 8$ =	___
E	$9 + 9 + 5 + 4$ =	___
F	$2 + 3 + 3 + 2$ =	___
G	$6 + 7 + 8 + 2$ =	___
H	$4 + 3 + 5 + 2$ =	___
I	$8 + 8 + 4 + 8$ =	___
K	$3 + 4 + 2 + 2$ =	___
L	$5 + 3 + 2 + 5$ =	___
M	$7 + 6 + 7 + 6$ =	___
N	$6 + 3 + 9 + 6$ =	___
O	$2 + 6 + 4 + 1$ =	___
P	$9 + 3 + 3 + 3$ =	___
R	$5 + 5 + 5 + 5$ =	___
S	$9 + 9 + 5 + 6$ =	___
T	$4 + 2 + 3 + 3$ =	___
U	$7 + 7 + 5 + 3$ =	___
V	$7 + 3 + 5 + 2$ =	___
Y	$3 + 7 + 4 + 7$ =	___

Which Way?

Samuel the prophet wanted to guide the children of Israel to the Lord. Find the correct way through the maze to the Lord.

Serve the Lord

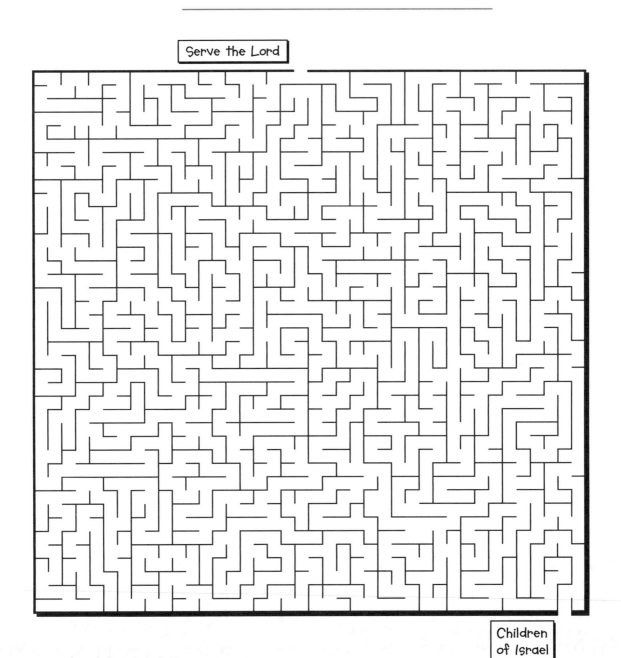

Children of Israel

Burdens

King Solomon had put a heavy burden on the children of Israel. His son Rehoboam was asked to ease the heavy burden. His reply to the people of Israel helped to divide the kingdom into two parts.

Find the letter code by filling in the answers below.

How many:

A Pennies in a quarter? ☐   **C** Days in a week? ☐   **D** Months in a year? ☐

E Books in the Bible? ☐   **F** Pennies in a nickel? ☐   **G** Feet in a yard? ☐

H Wings on a bird? ☐   **I** Years in a decade? ☐   **K** Nickels in a dollar? ☐

L Inches in a yard? ☐   **M** Ounces in a pound? ☐   **N** Days in September? ☐

O Quarts in a gallon? ☐   **P** Weeks in a year? ☐   **R** Minutes in an hour? ☐

S Pennies in two quarters? ☐   **T** Pennies in three nickels? ☐

U Hours in a day? ☐   **V** Books in the Old Testament? ☐

W Dimes in four dollars? ☐   **Y** Books in the New Testament? ☐

"
__ __ __ __ __ __ __ __ __ __ __ __ __ __ __ __ __ __ __ __ __ __ __ __ __ ;
16 27   5 25 15 2 66 60   16 25 12 66   27 4 24 60   27 4 20 66   2 66 25 39 27

__   __ __ __ __ __   __ __ __ __   __ __   __ __ __ __   __ __ __ __ __ __ __ __   __ __ .
10   40 10 36 36   16 25 20 66   10 15   66 39 66 30   2 66 25 39 10 66 60   16 27

__ __ __ __ __ __   __ __ __ __ __ __ __ __   __ __ __   __ __ __ __   __ __ __ __ __ __ ;
5 25 15 2 66 60   50 7 4 24 60 3 66 12   27 4 24   40 10 15 2   40 2 10 52 50   10

__ __ __ __ __   __ __ __ __ __ __   __ __ __   __ __ __ __   __ __ __ __ __ __ __ __ __ . "
40 10 36 36   50 7 4 24 60 3 66   27 4 24   40 10 15 2   50 7 4 60 52 10 4 30 50

(1 Kings 12:14)

Lost Kingdom

Add 7 to each number to complete the code.

A	B	C	D	E	F	G	H	I	J	K	L	M
17	38	41	54	92	72	12	25	32	63	58	27	36

N	O	P	Q	R	S	T	U	V	W	X	Y	Z
84	77	15	21	30	62	89	46	19	39	51	68	71

Jeroboam became king of the northern kingdom, which was called Israel. He didn't follow the Lord's commands but led the people into worshiping false gods. What did the prophet Ahijah say God would do because of Jeroboam's choices?

"

___ ___ ___   ___ ___   ___ ___ ___ ___   ___ ___ ___ ___
24 91 61   32 99   46 39 34 34   19 39 26 99

___ ___ ___ ___ ___ ___   ___ ___   ___ ___ ___ ___ ___ ___ ___
39 69 37 24 99 34   53 22   45 99 48 24 53 69 99

___ ___   ___ ___ ___   ___ ___ ___ ___   ___ ___ ___ ___ ___ ___ ___ ___
84 79   96 32 99   69 39 91 69   70 99 37 84 45 84 24 43

___ ___ ___   ___ ___ ___ ___ ___ ___ ___ ___ ___   ___ ___ ___
32 24 69   48 84 43 43 39 96 96 99 61   24 91 61

"

___ ___ ___   ___ ___ ___ ___ ___ ___ ___   ___ ___ ___ ___ ___ ___   ___ ___   ___ ___ ___ ___ ___ ___
32 24 69   48 24 53 69 99 61   39 69 37 24 99 34   96 84   48 84 43 43 39 96

(1 Kings 14:16)

Breakfast with the Birds

Elijah told wicked King Ahab that there would be no rain in Israel for several years. Then Elijah went into hiding to save his life. Write the letter that comes two letters before the letter given to discover the strange menu God provided for Elijah while he was in hiding.

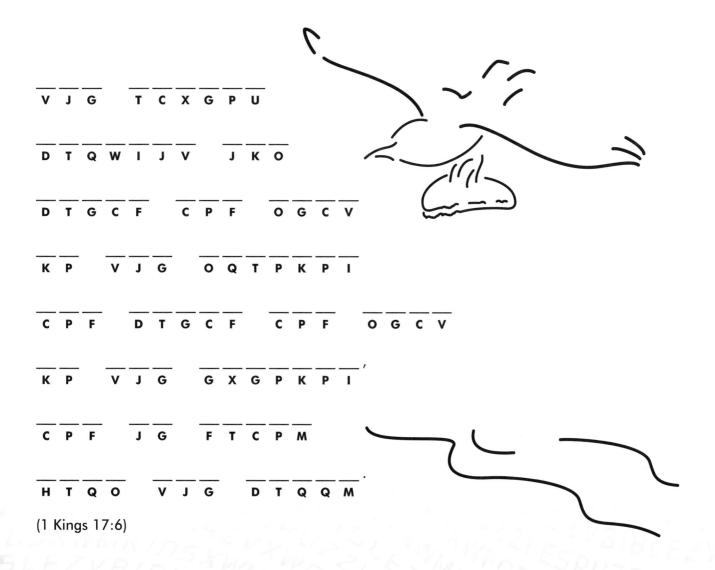

V J G   T C X G P U

D T Q W I J V   J K O

D T G C F   C P F   O G C V

K P   V J G   O Q T P K I

C P F   D T G C F   C P F   O G C V

K P   V J G   G X G P K I '

C P F   J G   F T C P M

H T Q O   V J G   D T Q Q M .

(1 Kings 17:6)

A Prayer for Healing

Elisha was called because a Shunammite woman's son had died. Following the Lord's directions, what strange method did Elisha use to bring the boy back to life?

A	=	01
E	=	05
I	=	09
O	=	15
U	=	21

Find out how Elisha did it by filling in the letters below. Part of the code has been given to you.

___ ___   ___ ___ ___ ___   ___ ___ '   ___ ___ ___ ___   ___ ___ ___   ___ ___ ___ ___   ___ ___   ___ ___ ___
08 05   23 05 14 20   09 14   19 08 21 20   20 08 05   04 15 15 18   15 14   20 08 05

___ ___ ___   ___ ___   ___ ___ ___ ___ ___   ___ ___ ___   ___ ___ ___ ___ ___ ___   ___ ___   ___ ___ ___ ___ ___
20 23 15   15 06   20 08 05 13   01 14 04   16 18 01 25 05 04   20 15   20 08 05

___ ___ ___ ___ .   ___ ___ ___ ___ ___   ___ ___   ___ ___ ___   ___ ___   ___ ___ ___ ___ ___   ___ ___ ___   ___ ___ ___
12 15 18 04   20 08 05 14   08 05   07 15 20   15 14   20 08 05   02 05 04   01 14 04

___ ___ ___   ___ ___ ___ ___ ___   ___ ___ ___ ___ ___   ___ ___ ___ '   ___ ___ ___ ___ ___   ___ ___   ___ ___ ___ ___ ___ '
12 01 25   21 16 15 14   20 08 05   02 15 25   13 15 21 20 08   20 15   13 15 21 20 08

___ ___ ___ ___   ___ ___   ___ ___ ___ ___ '   ___ ___ ___ ___ ___   ___ ___   ___ ___ ___ ___ ___ .   ___ ___   ___ ___ ___
05 25 05 19   20 15   05 25 05 19   08 01 14 04 19   20 15   08 01 14 04 19   01 19   08 05

___ ___ ___ ___ ___ ___ ___ ___ ___   ___ ___ ___ ___ ___ ___ ___   ___ ___ ___   ___ ___ ___ ___   ___ ___ ___ '
19 20 18 05 20 03 08 05 04   08 09 13 19 05 12 06   15 21 20   21 16 15 14   08 09 13

___ ___ ___   ___ ___ ___ ___ '___   ___ ___ ___ ___   ___ ___ ___ ___   ___ ___ ___ ___ .   (2 Kings 4:33, 34)
20 08 05   02 15 25 19   02 15 04 25   07 18 05 23   23 01 18 13

Words of Wisdom

Solomon's words of wisdom found in Proverbs 3:5, 6 still speak to us today. Discover his words by filling in the open crossword puzzle. When you are finished, use the words to fill in the blanks and complete the Scripture.

3 letters	5 letters
NOT	TRUST
ALL	HEART
HIM	PATHS
OWN	
	8 letters
4 letters	STRAIGHT
LORD	
LEAN	11 letters
YOUR	ACKNOWLEDGE
WAYS	
WILL	13 letters
MAKE	UNDERSTANDING

_____ in the _____ with all your _____ and _____

_____ on _____ _____ _____ ;

in _____ your _____ _____ _____ ,

and he _____ _____ your _____ _____ .

Restore the Temple

Use the code to discover how the people reacted to King Joash's proclamation.

One hundred and two years had passed since Solomon had died, and the temple had fallen into disrepair. Joash became the king when he was 7 years old. Years later he decided to restore the temple. He issued a proclamation in Judah and Jerusalem that everyone should bring to the Lord the tax that Moses had required of Israel (2 Chronicles 24:8-14).

```
___ ___ ___    ___ ___ ___    ___ ___ ___ ___ ___ ___    ___ ___ ___
 6  15  15     4  14  8      7  8  16  7  15  8      6  11  1

___ ___ ___ ___ ___ ___ ___ ___ ___    ___ ___ ___ ___ ___ ___    ___ ___ ___ ___ ___ ___ ___
16  20  20  9  13  9  6  15  19     2  15  6  1  15  5      18  12  16  10  2  14  4

___ ___ ___ ___ ___    ___ ___ ___ ___ ___ ___ ___ ___ ___ ___
 4  14  8  9  12      16  20  20  8  12  9  11  2  19

___ ___ ___    ___ ___ ___ ___ ___ ___ ___
 6  11  1      1  12  16  7  7  8  1

___ ___ ___ ___    ___ ___    ___ ___ ___
 4  14  8  3      9  11      4  14  8

___ ___ ___ ___ ___    ___ ___ ___ ___ ___
13  14  8  19  4     10  11  4  9  15

___ ___    ___ ___ ___    ___ ___ ___ ___ .
 9  4      17  6  19     20  10  15  15
```

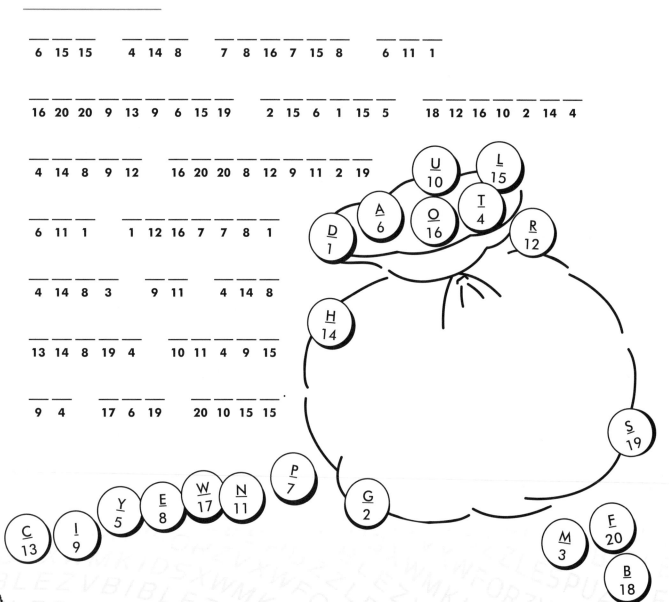

A Petition and a Request

Use the code to decipher the message by writing the opposite letter on the lines provided. Example: for the letter C, *P* would be the answer.

A	B	C	D	E	F	G	H	I	J	K	L	M
N	O	P	Q	R	S	T	U	V	W	X	Y	Z

Wicked Haman plotted to kill all of the Jews throughout the kingdom of Xerxes. Queen Esther brought a petition to the king for her people. Use the code to discover Esther's request (Esther 3:5, 6; 7:1-4).

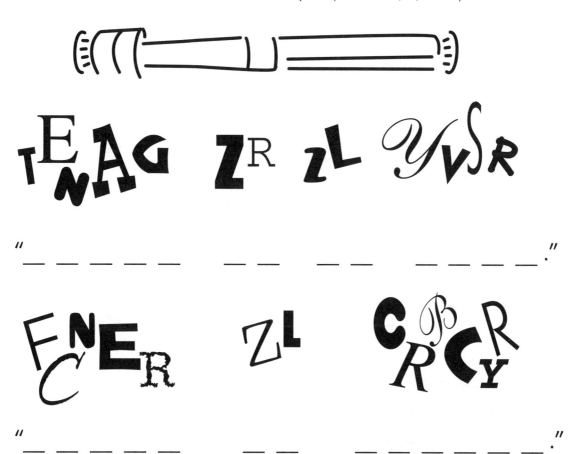

TENAG   ZR   ZL   YVSR

" _ _ _ _ _   _ _   _ _   _ _ _ _ . "

FNER   ZL   CRBCR

" _ _ _ _   _ _   _ _ _ _ _ _ . "

Psalm of Numbers

A = 23, 34, 40, 61 72, 89
B = 29, 77
D = 7, 19, 49, 73, 81
E = 3, 14, 17, 30, 38, 42, 45,
    48, 57, 58, 66, 69, 71,
    76, 78, 82, 86, 91, 95,
    97, 102
G = 55
H = 2, 13, 16, 22, 37, 68, 94
I = 8, 20, 31, 47, 53, 80, 85
K = 41
L = 4, 24, 25, 46, 70, 109

M = 10, 39, 44, 75, 104
N = 26, 32, 35, 52, 54, 59
O = 5, 27, 50, 100, 107
P = 15, 60
Q = 83
R = 6, 18, 56, 65, 92, 96, 101
S = 9, 12, 21, 43, 62, 67, 74,
    79, 93, 98, 103, 106
T = 1, 28, 36, 63, 87, 90, 99
U = 64, 84, 108
W = 33, 51, 88
Y = 11, 105

Psalm 23:1-3 is hidden among the numbers.
To discover its message, transfer each letter
to every number listed beside it.

___ ___ ___   ___ ___ ___ ___   ___ ___   ___ ___   ___ ___ ___ ___ ___ ___ ___ ___ ___ ___ ,   ___
1 2 3   4 5 6 7   8 9   10 11   12 13 14 15 16 17 18 19   20

___ ___ ___ ___ ___   ___ ___ ___   ___ ___   ___ ___   ___ ___ ___ ___   ___ ___   ___ ___ ___ ___ ___ .
21 22 23 24 25   26 27 28   29 30   31 32   33 34 35 36   37 38   39 40 41 42 43

___ ___   ___ ___ ___   ___ ___ ___ ___   ___ ___   ___ ___ ___ ___ ___   ___ ___ ___ ___ ___ ___ ___ ___ ,
44 45   46 47 48   49 50 51 52   53 54   55 56 57 58 59   60 61 62 63 64 65 66 67

___ ___   ___ ___ ___ ___ ___   ___ ___   ___ ___ ___ ___ ___ ___   ___ ___ ___ ___ ___
68 69   70 71 72 73 74   75 76   77 78 79 80 81 82   83 84 85 86 87

___ ___ ___ ___ ___ ___ ,   ___ ___   ___ ___ ___ ___ ___ ___ ___ ___   ___ ___   ___ ___ ___ ___ .
88 89 90 91 92 93   94 95   96 97 98 99 100101102103   104105   106107108109

The Earth Praises God

The words of Psalm 66:1, 2 are hidden in the diagram. Find the words by matching the shapes of the upper boxes to the shapes of the lower boxes. Then write the letters in the lower boxes. When all the boxes have been matched, write the letters from left to right on the lines below.

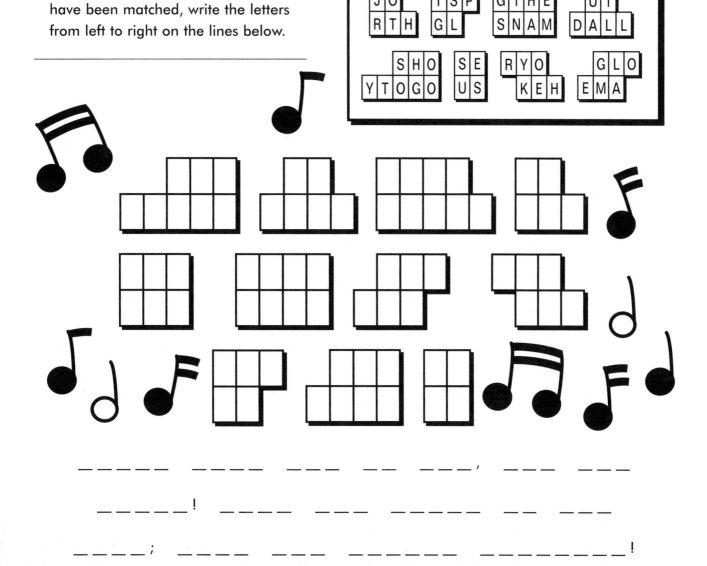

____ ____ ___ __ ___' ___ ___

_____! ____ ___ ____ __ ___

____; ____ ___ _____ _____!

God Created the Earth

Psalm 104:5 is hidden among the letters. Find the message by writing the lowercase letters on the lines provided.

		C	h				
		e	N				
	s	e	E	t	t	A	
	h	e	R	e	a	L	
r	t	F	h	o	n	P	i	t	Q
s	f	o	u	M	E	N	d	a	D
t	i	o	U	n	G	s	i	t	A	c	a	B	n
n	e	v	I	E	r	b	e	m	o	R	v	e	d

__ ___ ___ _____ __ _____ __

___ _____ ; __

___ _____ __ _____ .

The Word of God

The words of Psalm 119:11 are hidden in the cryptogram.
Use the code to decipher the message.

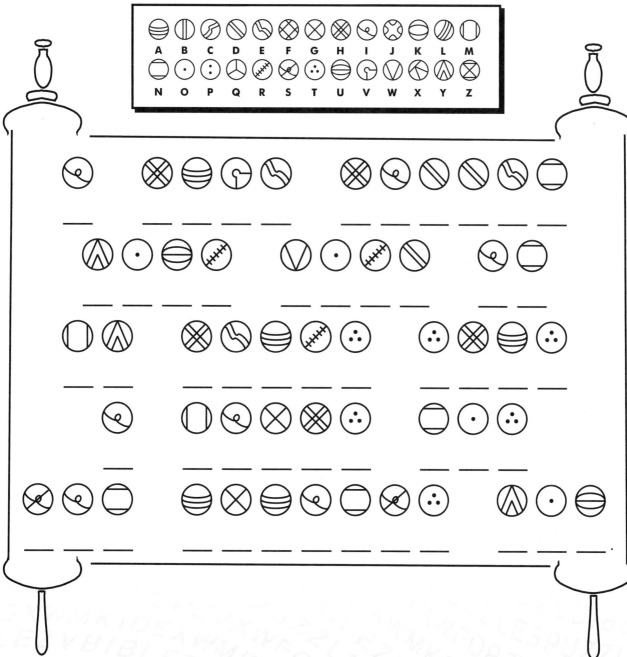

Which Way to Go?

The confusion of signs holds an important message.
To discover what the signs say, start at the first set of signs on
the left side of the page and read the signs down the pole, then
progress to the next pole. If the sign points left, then count the
letters from right to left and record the correct letters on the
lines. If the sign points right, count the letters from left to right.

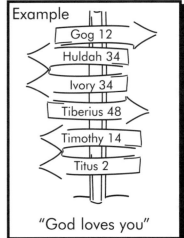

Example

Gog 12
Huldah 34
Ivory 34
Tiberius 48
Timothy 14
Titus 2

"God loves you"

Isaiah prophesied about the
birth of Jesus. He said the
Lord himself would give them
a sign. What was the sign?
(Isaiah 7:14)

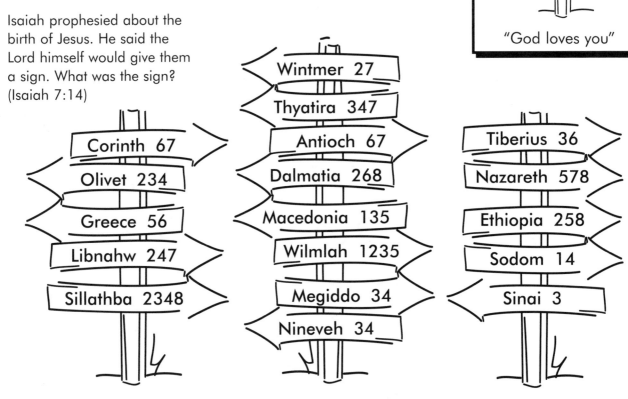

Corinth 67
Olivet 234
Greece 56
Libnahw 247
Sillathba 2348

Wintmer 27
Thyatira 347
Antioch 67
Dalmatia 268
Macedonia 135
Wilmlah 1235
Megiddo 34
Nineveh 34

Tiberius 36
Nazareth 578
Ethiopia 258
Sodom 14
Sinai 3

"_ _ _   _ _ _ _   _ _ _   _ _ _   _ _

_ _ _   _ _ _ _   _ _ _ _   _ _   _ _ _ _."

God's Choice

Use the code wheel to decipher what God spoke to Jeremiah (Jeremiah 18:7, 8).

" __ __ . . . __   __ __ __ __ __ __ __ __
  13 22   13   9 25 25 3 6 25 10 11

__ __ __ __   __   __ __ __ __ __ __   __ __
18 24 9 18   9   25 9 18 13 3 25   3 21

__ __ __ __ __ __ __   __ __   __ __   __ __ __
1 13 25 12 16 3 2   13 5   18 3   19 11

. . . __ __ __ __ __ __ __ __ __ , __ __ __   __ __
     16 11 5 18 21 3 8 11 16   9 25 16   13 22

__ __ __ __   __ __ __ __ __ __ . . . __ __ __ __ __ __
18 24 9 18   25 9 18 13 3 25   21 11 15 11 25 18 5

__ __   __ __ __ __ , __ __ __ __   __ __   __ __ __ __
3 22   13 18 5   11 26 13 17   18 24 11 25   13   7 13 17 17

__ __ __ __ __ __   __ __ __   __ __ __   __ __ __ __ __ __ __ __   __ __   __ __ __
21 11 17 11 25 18   9 25 16   25 3 18   13 25 22 17 13 10 18   3 25   13 18

__ __ __ __   __ __ __ __ __ __ __ __   __   __ __ __   __ __ __ __ __ __ __ __ . "
18 24 11   16 13 5 9 5 18 11 21   13   24 9 16   15 17 9 25 25 11 16

I Have Plans for You

God spoke to Jeremiah about the future of Israel in Jeremiah 29:11. Follow the instructions to discover what God told him.

Use the code to interpret the message. The first letter of the code represents the vertical column and the second letter, the horizontal column. For example, *DF* would be the letter *W*.

	A	D	F	G	V	X
A	F	L	1	A	O	2
D	J	D	W	3	G	U
F	C	I	Y	B	4	P
G	R	5	Q	8	V	E
V	6	K	7	Z	M	X
X	S	N	H	O	T	9

"__ __ __   __   __ __ __ __   __ __ __   __ __ __ __ __
AA AV GA   FD   VD XD AV DF   XV XF GX   FX AD AG XD XA

__   __ __ __ __   __ __ __   __ __ __,"   __ __ __ __ __ __ __
FD   XF AG GV GX   AA AV GA   FF AV DX   DD GX FA AD AG GA GX XA

__ __ __   __ __ __ __,   "__ __ __ __ __   __ __   __ __ __ __ __ __
XV XF GX   AD AV GA DD   FX AD AG XD XA   XV AV   FX GA AV XA FX GX GA

__ __ __   __ __ __   __ __ __   __ __   __ __ __ __   __ __ __,
FF AV DX   AG XD DD   XD AV XV   XV AV   XF AG GA VV   FF AV DX

__ __ __ __ __   __ __   __ __ __ __   __ __ __   __ __ __ __
FX AD AG XD XA   XV AV   DV FD GV GX   FF AV DX   XF AV FX GX

__ __ __   __   __ __ __ __ __ __ __."
AG XD DD   AG   AA DX XV DX GA GX

Good Things to Eat

Daniel was taken into captivity, along with other Israelites, to Babylon. He was chosen as one of the young men from the royal family who were without physical defect, handsome, smart, well informed, and quick to understand. The king ordered food and drink to be given to the young men from his own table, but Daniel requested different food. What kind of food did he request?

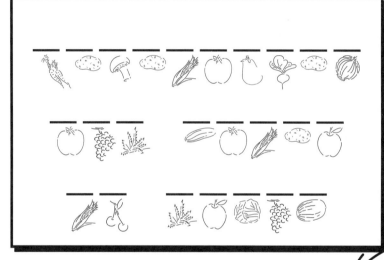

Find the answer by comparing the small food items with the ones in the group picture. Locate the letter in the group picture and transfer it to the lines provided.

Daniel and the Lions

Daniel told King Darius that God had shut the mouths of the lions. Why did he say that?

To find the answer, start on the lion's forehead and travel through the maze, recording every other letter on the lines provided. When you have reached the last letter, follow the arrow to the next letter to be recorded. Record every other letter as you work your way back through the maze.

_____ ___ _____

_____ __ ___'_ _____'

___ ___ __ ____ ____

___ _____ _____ ____

_____ .

Repent or Be Destroyed

The Lord instructed Jonah to preach
to Nineveh. To find out how his message
affected the citizens of Nineveh, follow the directions below.

Find the letters of the left-column words in the middle column and cross them out.
Write the remaining letters on the lines in the right column. When finished, read
the beginning part of the message, then move down the words in the left column,
followed by the words in the right column.

The king of Nineveh put on sackcloth and declared that . . .

NO ONE	NOONONE	_ _
SHOULD	SHOTUHLDE	_ _ _
EAT	LEORATD	_ _ _ _
OR	OANRD	_ _ _
DRINK,	DRIGINKVE	_ _ _ _
BUT	BUUTP	_ _
EVERYONE	EVTHEREYOIRNE	_ _ _ _ _
SHOULD	SHEOVUILLD	_ _ _ _
CALL	WCAALYLS	_ _ _ _ .

Bible Story Word Hunt

Word List

AFRAID
ANGEL
BABY
ELIZABETH
GABRIEL
GOD
JOHN
JOY
PRAYER
PRIEST
SILENT
SON
SPEAK
TABLET
TEMPLE
ZECHARIAH

Important words from the Bible story of John's birth are hidden in this word hunt. See how many you can find, reading forward and backward, up and down, and diagonally.

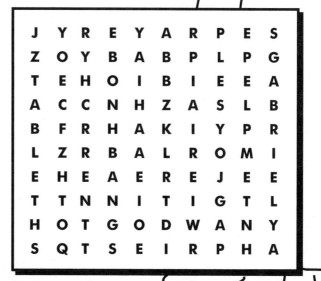

```
J  Y  R  E  Y  A  R  P  E  S
Z  O  Y  B  A  B  P  L  P  G
T  E  H  O  I  B  I  E  E  A
A  C  C  N  H  Z  A  S  L  B
B  F  R  H  A  K  I  Y  P  R
L  Z  R  B  A  L  R  O  M  I
E  H  E  A  E  R  E  J  E  E
T  T  N  N  I  T  I  G  T  L
H  O  T  G  O  D  W  A  N  Y
S  Q  T  S  E  I  R  P  H  A
```

Stable Mates

A stable? It was a strange birthplace for a king! But the Bible tells us that is where Mary and Joseph spent the night when Jesus was born. Scripture also tells us that shepherds came. Now think about that night. Who else could have been there?

Unscramble each set of letters in the stable and write your answer on its line.

Syllable Stumpers

Here are some questions about Luke 2:21-40. You can build your answers with letters from the Syllable Box. The number of syllables needed is in parenthesis. The number of letters is shown by blank lines. (Remember: each syllable is used once, so cross out each one as you use it.)

Syllable Box

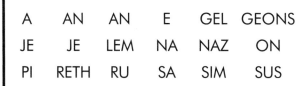

A	AN	AN	E	GEL	GEONS
JE	JE	LEM	NA	NAZ	ON
PI	RETH	RU	SA	SIM	SUS

1. Who told Mary and Joseph what to name their baby? (2) __ __ __ __ __

2. What did they name their baby? (2) __ __ __ __ __

3. Mary and Joseph traveled to what city? (4) __ __ __ __ __ __ __ __ __ __

4. What offering did they bring to the temple? (2) __ __ __ __ __ __ __

5. Who was the faithful man at the temple? (3) __ __ __ __ __ __

6. Who was the prophetess at the temple? (2) __ __ __ __

7. When Mary and Joseph went home, where did they go? (3) __ __ __ __ __ __ __ __

Wise Men
—Matthew 2

The Gifts of Kings

The kings followed a star to Bethlehem, and they brought their gifts to Jesus. It is thought that this event may have inspired today's custom of Christmas giving.

Read the three gift descriptions that follow. Then, to see what the gifts mean, write the first letter of picture names in the blanks.

---

1. This gift from deep in the earth could have been shaped as a beautiful bowl, a crown of jewels, coins, or a shiny statue. . . . GOLD

It is the symbol of ___ ___ ___ ___ ___ ___ .

---

2. This gift, burned, was collected as sap from a tree that grows in Africa and Asia. . . . INCENSE

It is the symbol of ___ ___ ___ ___ ___ .

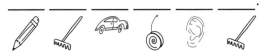

---

3. This gift, used in perfume and embalming, started out as a gummy substance from a bush. . . . MYRRH

It is the symbol of ___ ___ ___ ___ ___ ___ ___ ___ .

On the Trail

In this box of letters, trace over the trail that spells out the second question Jesus asked. (Move right, left, up, down, or diagonally.)

When Jesus was 12, He traveled with His parents to Jerusalem for the Feast of the Passover. After the feast, Jesus stayed behind.

His parents searched and searched and finally found Him in the temple. Jesus asked them why they were searching. He also asked them another question.

Start

D	O	T	Y	P	A	K	B	
I	N	M	L	O	U	N	K	K
D	H	B	O	I	J	O	W	
O	B	E	A	T	G	F	I	
M	N	I	D	E	D	A	H	
Y	C	A	B	H	E	R	A	
G	F	H	T	U	O	H	S	
F	E	D	E	S	C	B	A	

Wilderness Maze

After Jesus was baptized, He went into the wilderness for 40 days. There, the devil tempted Him three times, but Jesus did not give in.

Find the path that takes Jesus through the devil's temptations and out into the world to begin His ministry. Write the words you find along the path in order on the lines below to find two responses Jesus made to Satan.

(Luke 4:8, 12)

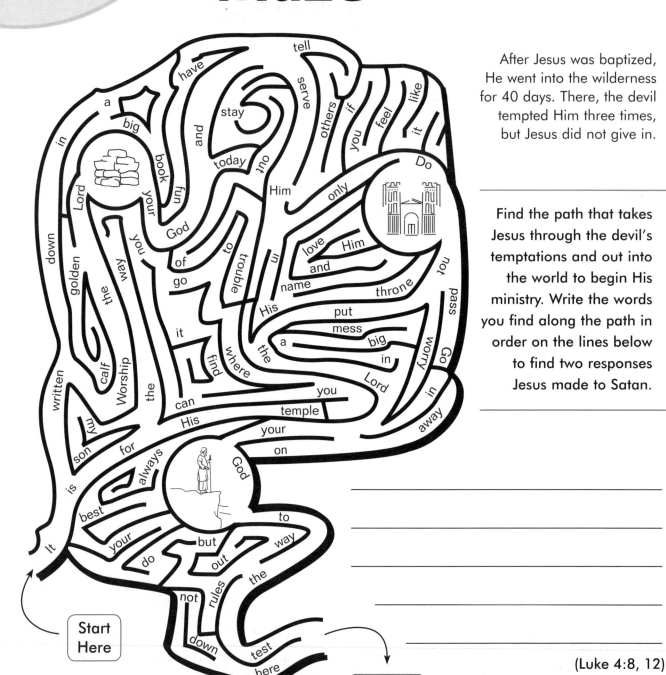

Start Here

Ministry

Disciple Kriss Kross

Look up Matthew 10:2-4 to get the facts. Then fill in the 12 disciples' names in the puzzle.

My Father's House

Jesus was angry when He saw the house of the Lord used as a market for buying and selling. Use details from both stories (Matthew 21:12, 13; John 2:13-16) to solve the crossword puzzle.

CLUES

1. The largest animals sold in the temple were _____.
2. Where in the temple did the selling take place?
3. The temple was in the city of _____.
4. In this story, it is almost time for the Jewish holiday of _____.
5. The smallest animals sold in the temple were _____.
6. In the story, what did Jesus make from cords?
7. In the temple, those who traded one type of money for another were called money _____.
8. Name another animal sold in the temple.
9. Jesus said the temple was to be a "house of _____."
10. What did Jesus tip over?
11. Jesus said that the temple was not supposed to be a "den of _____."

A Bible Verse for Everyone

In the puzzle, there is a special place for every word in this Scripture. All shared letters have been filled in for you to give you a good start. Can you find the right fit?

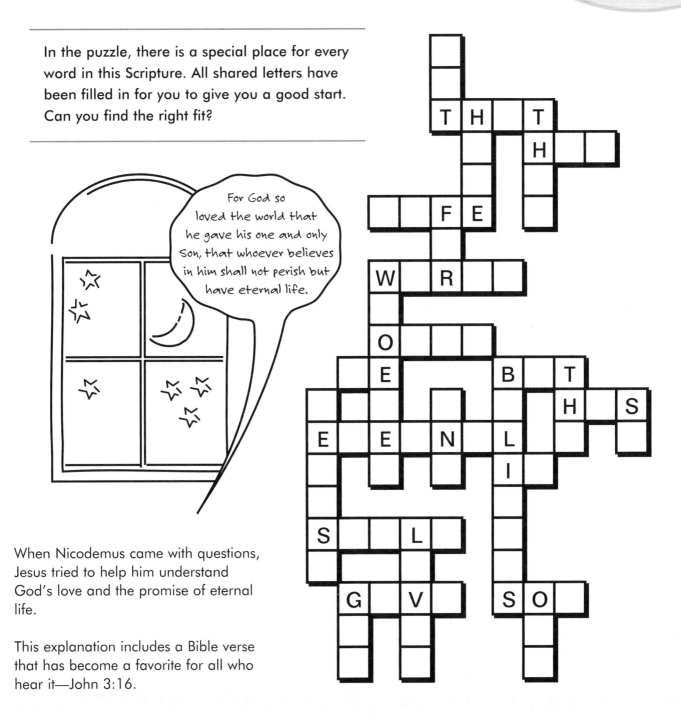

For God so loved the world that he gave his one and only Son, that whoever believes in him shall not perish but have eternal life.

When Nicodemus came with questions, Jesus tried to help him understand God's love and the promise of eternal life.

This explanation includes a Bible verse that has become a favorite for all who hear it—John 3:16.

Circle Search

Hidden in this circle are 10 different health problems that Jesus healed during His ministry on earth. Write them in a list as you find them. Can you think of others? Add them to the bottom of the list.

1. _____
2. _____
3. _____
4. _____
5. _____
6. _____
7. _____
8. _____
9. _____
10. _____

EXTRAS

_____
_____
_____
_____
_____

CRIPPLEDEFDEADGBHPARALYZEDISJDEAFKLMUTEMNBLINDOPINSANEQRBLEEDINGSTBLEPERANSICKOB

START

Following Jesus

The apostles are ready to follow Jesus. They want to learn from Him and help Him in His ministry. Can you help them find the right path? Mark the route. There's only one right way to go!

1   2   3   4

Beatitude Reflections

You will need something extra to solve this puzzle. Hold your puzzle up in front of a mirror to read its reflection. Doing this will turn the backwards print around.

Then draw lines to connect each Beatitude beginning with its reflected ending. Need help? Check Matthew 5:1-12.

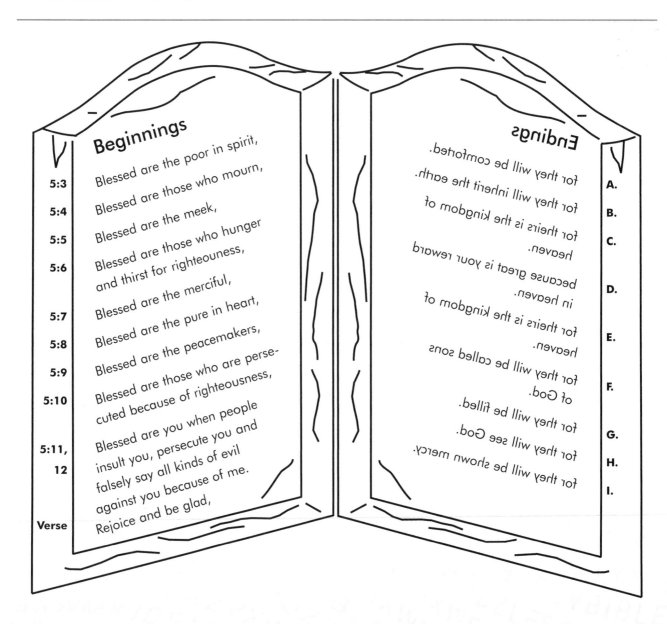

Beginnings

Verse	
5:3	Blessed are the poor in spirit,
5:4	Blessed are those who mourn,
5:5	Blessed are the meek,
5:6	Blessed are those who hunger and thirst for righteouness,
5:7	Blessed are the merciful,
5:8	Blessed are the pure in heart,
5:9	Blessed are the peacemakers,
5:10	Blessed are those who are perse-cuted because of righteousness,
5:11, 12	Blessed are you when people insult you, persecute you and falsely say all kinds of evil against you because of me. Rejoice and be glad,

Endings

A. for they will be comforted.
B. for they will inherit the earth.
C. for theirs is the kingdom of heaven.
D. because great is your reward in heaven.
E. for theirs is the kingdom of heaven.
F. for they will be called sons of God.
G. for they will be filled.
H. for they will see God.
I. for they will be shown mercy.

One Square at a Time

Copy the squares below onto the grid to make this Prayer Reminder. When you finish, you may use pencils or markers to color it. Remember that God is a good listener. He wants to hear our prayers.

Jesus taught the people a special prayer.

"Our Father in heaven, hallowed be your name, your kingdom come, your will be done on earth as it is in heaven.
Give us today our daily bread.
Forgive us our debts, as we also have forgiven our debtors.
And lead us not into temptation, but deliver us from the evil one." (Matthew 6:9-13)

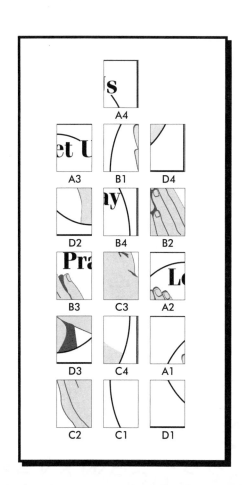

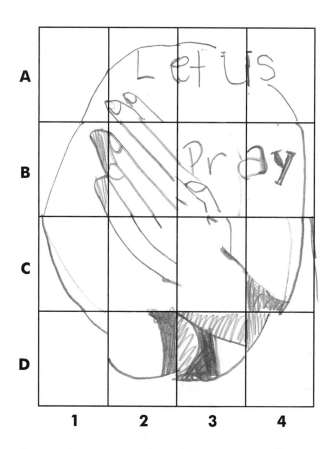

Vanishing Letters

The printer is running out of ink! Use a pencil to fix the letters that aren't all there, and you will have a rhyming reminder of this Bible story. Look in Matthew 7:24-29 if you need help.

Be a Builder

If a builder you would be,
Don't build on shifting sand.
For when the wind and rain beat down
Your house will never stand!

But if construction is your game,
Build on the rock that's strong,
For then your house will stand the storm
All day and all night long.

Be a builder—a better builder—
In all you say and do.
Be a builder—a better builder—
For the Lord asks this of you.

Story Grid Fill-in

In this puzzle, color all the spaces containing letters needed to spell the word FAITH, and see the answer appear.

The centurion believed that Jesus could heal his sick servant with only a word! And Jesus saw that this man had great faith. Jesus hopes to see our faith in Him too.

E	K	C	Q	J	P	N	X	B	W	O	D	W	L	V	J	R	K	X	E	B
L	T	A	I	R	H	A	F/L	C	T	P	F	K	H	A	T	O	I	H	F	J
B	G	F	O	E	A	K	I	M	I	J	A	E	C	A/F/C/O/T	J/H/P/G	F/D/I	C	G	T	Q	M
M	D	H	C	J	T	F	T/E	D	A	N	T	B					D	J	F	O	C
P	N	A	V	W	F	B/A/K		L	F	H	I	O	F	T	F	M	E	A	K	N
C	K	R	D	B	G	L	P	J	M	E	G	C	K	Q	N	V	B	L	P	D

Having faith means we _____ Jesus.

Will It Grow?

Add the numbers in the box to get the code number for each letter. Then solve the puzzle.

Farmers plant seeds in all types of soils. Fertilizer is used in order to grow a good crop. But the question is still there—will it grow? Christians spread the Word of God to all types of listeners. What is necessary for the seed of faith to grow in each person's heart?

A $17+34 =$ ____

B $28+44 =$ ____

C $39+57 =$ ____

D $16+65 =$ ____

E $62+37 =$ ____

F $41+38 =$ ____

G $24+33 =$ ____

H $47+29 =$ ____

I $24+58 =$ ____

L $41+25 =$ ____

N $23+15 =$ ____

O $29+49 =$ ____

P $22+11 =$ ____

R $55+34 =$ ____

S $29+16 =$ ____

T $44+26 =$ ____

U $13+14 =$ ____

V $23+68 =$ ____

W $23+19 =$ ____

Y $36+25 =$ ____

"
__ __ __   __ __ __   __ __ __ __   __ __
72 27 70   70 76 99   45 99 99 81   78 38

__ __ __ __   __ __ __ __   __ __ __ __ __
57 78 78 81   45 78 82 66   45 70 51 38 81 45

__ __ __   __ __ __ __ __   __ __ __ __   __
79 78 89   70 76 78 45 99   42 82 70 76   51

__ __ __ __ __   __ __ __   __ __ __ __
38 78 72 66 99   51 38 81   57 78 78 81

__ __ __ __ __,   __ __ __   __ __ __ __ __   __ __ __
76 99 51 89 70   42 76 78   76 99 51 89   70 76 99

__ __ __ __,   __ __ __ __ __ __   __ __,   __ __ __
42 78 89 81   89 99 70 51 82 38   82 70   51 38 81

__ __   __ __ __ __ __ __ __ __ __ __ __ __
72 61   33 99 89 45 99 91 99 89 82 38 57

__ __ __ __ __ __ __   __   __ __ __ __." (Luke 8:15)
33 89 78 81 27 96 99   51   96 89 78 33

Jesus Calms the Sea
—Matthew 8

In Morse code, SOS is a call for help. Jesus and His disciples were on the Sea of Galilee when a furious storm came up on the lake. The disciples immediately went to Jesus for help. What miraculous way did Jesus use to save His disciples from the storm?

Use the letter code to find out what Jesus did. The first word has been completed as an example.

A	B	C	D	E	F	G	H	I	J	K	L	M
F	M	H	Q	L	Y	P	V	N	U	R	D	J

N	O	P	Q	R	S	T	U	V	W	X	Y	Z
C	T	I	A	W	K	E	Z	S	G	O	B	X

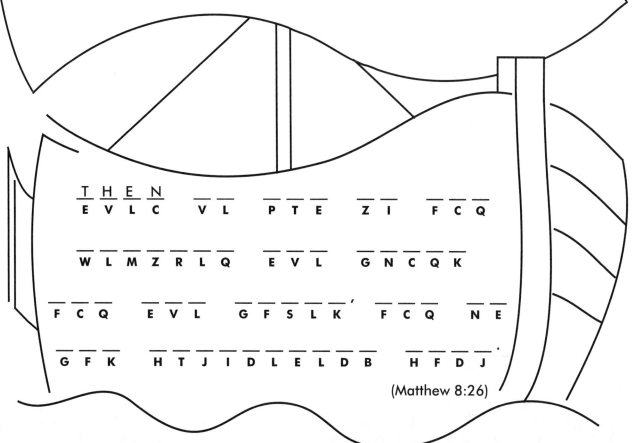

T H E N ____ ____ ____ ____ ____
E V L C   V L   P T E   Z I   F C Q

____ ____ ____
W L M Z R L Q   E V L   G N C Q K

____ ____ ____' ____ ____
F C Q   E V L   G F S L K   F C Q   N E

____ ____ ____.
G F K   H T J I D L E L D B   H F D J

(Matthew 8:26)

A Timely Healing

Jesus confronted a man possessed by evil spirits. He drove the evil spirits into a herd of pigs. The pigs rushed down a bank and into a lake and were drowned. Jesus has power over sin, death, and the devil. Use the timely code to discover what Jesus wanted the healed man to do.

for - Six thirty-eight = _____
on - Three fifty-six = _____
has - One forty-eight = _____
he - Six fifty-two = _____
had - Four twenty-seven = _____
Lord - Eight twenty-five = _____
to - Ten fifty-six = _____
done - Ten forty-three = _____
has - One thirty-two = _____
tell - Nine fifty-four = _____
how - Three twenty-five = _____
and - Five twenty-six = _____
family - Two twenty-six = _____
home - Eleven fourteen = _____
much - Seven twenty-nine = _____
how - Nine thirty = _____
them - Five thirty-four = _____
you - Four fifty-one = _____
mercy - Eight thirty-seven = _____
and - Seven fifty-nine = _____
the - Twelve nineteen = _____
you - Eleven thirty-eight = _____
your - Nine forty-one = _____
Go - Twelve thirty-four = _____

"
_____ _____ _____
12:34   11:14   10:56

_____ _____ _____
9:41   2:26   7:59

_____ _____ _____
9:54   5:34   3:25

_____ _____ _____
7:29   12:19   8:25

_____ _____ _____
1:48   10:43   6:38

_____ , _____ _____
4:51   5:26   9:30

_____ _____ _____
6:52   1:32   4:27

"
_____ _____ _____ _____.
8:37   3:56   11:38

(Mark 5:19)

Waste Not— Want Not

A	86 – 63 = ___
B	78 – 48 = ___
C	66 – 14 = ___
D	38 – 24 = ___
E	99 – 52 = ___
F	82 – 39 = ___
G	74 – 25 = ___
H	67 – 28 = ___
I	96 – 12 = ___
K	47 – 19 = ___
L	73 – 29 = ___
M	84 – 11 = ___
N	95 – 27 = ___
O	82 – 67 = ___
P	69 – 34 = ___
R	92 – 17 = ___
S	54 – 14 = ___
T	88 – 78 = ___
V	64 – 26 = ___
W	51 – 32 = ___
Y	99 – 10 = ___

Subtract the numbers in the box to get the code number for each letter. Then solve the puzzle.

Jesus used five small barley loaves and two small fish to feed over 5,000 people. What a wonderful miracle this was! Afterward, Jesus told His disciples to gather up what was left. He wanted nothing to be wasted. What miraculous sign happened then?

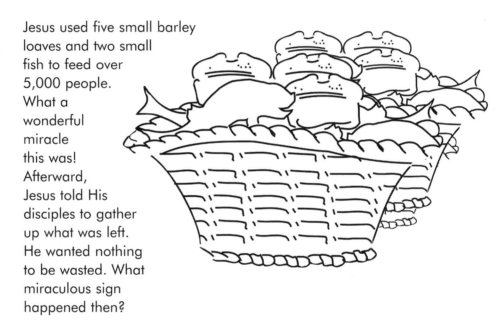

---
40 15   10 39 47 89   49 23 10 39 47 75 47 14   10 39 47 73   23 68 14

---
43 84 44 44 47 14   10 19 47 44 38 47   30 23 40 28 47 10 40   19 84 10 39

---
10 39 47   35 84 47 52 47 40   15 43   10 39 47   43 84 38 47   30 23 75 44 47 89

---
44 15 23 38 47 40   44 47 43 10   15 38 47 75   30 89   10 39 15 40 47   19 39 15

---
39 23 14   47 23 10 47 68 .   (John 6:13)

Two Meanings

The word *confession* may have two meanings. A confession may mean an admission of guilt. A confession may also mean a statement of belief. What type of confession did Simon Peter make? Jesus asked him, "Who do you say I am?"

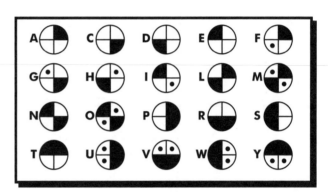

_____ _____ _____ _____ _____   _____ _____ _____ _____ _____

_____ _____ _____ _____ _____ _____ _____ , " _____ _____ _____

_____ _____ _____   _____ _____ _____   _____ _____ _____ _____ _____ ,

_____ _____ _____   _____ _____ _____   _____ _____

_____ _____ _____   _____ _____ _____ _____ _____   _____ _____ _____ ."

A Flash of Lightning

A flash of lightning may light up the entire sky. Jesus' clothes became as bright as a flash of lightning at His transfiguration. How are Jesus and a flash of lightning similar? Write the letter that comes between the two letters given to discover the light of Jesus.

___ ___ ___ ___ ___ ___ ___ ___ ___   ___ ___ ___ ___ ___ ___
KM HJ FH GI SU MO HJ MO FH   KM HJ FH GI SU RT

___ ___   ___ ___ ___   ___ ___ ___ ,   ___ ___ ___ ___ ___
TV OQ   SU GI DF   RT JL XZ   VX GI HJ KM DF

___ ___ ___ ___ ___   ___ ___ ___ ___ ___ ___   ___ ___ ___
IK DF RT TV RT   KM HJ FH GI SU RT   TV OQ

___ ___ ___   ___ ___ ___ ___ ___ ___   ___ ___ ___ ___ ___ .
NP TV QS   GI DF ZB QS SU RT   IK DF RT TV RT

___ ___   ___ ___ ___   ___ ___ ___ ___ ___
HJ RT   SU GI DF   KM HJ FH GI SU

___ ___ ___ ___   ___ ___ ___ ___ ___ ___
SU GI ZB SU   FH TV HJ CE DF RT

___ ___   ___ ___   ___ ___ ___
TV RT   SU NP   NP TV QS

___ ___ ___ ___ ___ ___ ___   ___ ___ ___ ___ .
GI DF ZB UW DF MO KM XZ   GI NP LN DF

Treating Others

Do the multiplication problems in the box to find out the code numbers for each letter.

The Parable of the Unmerciful Servant shows us how we should *not* treat others. But how does Jesus say we should treat others when they sin against us?

A	Three fours = ____
B	Seven sixes = ____
E	Nine nines = ____
F	Eight fours = ____
G	Five sevens = ____
H	Five threes = ____
I	Six fives = ____
M	Seven nines = ____
O	Four fours = ____
R	Eight nines = ____
T	Seven sevens = ____
U	Four sixes = ____
V	Nine fives = ____
Y	Five fours = ____

"____ ____ ____ ____ ____ ____ ____
32 16 72 35 30 45 81

____ ____ ____ ____
20 16 24 72

____ ____ ____ ____ ____ ____ ____
42 72 16 49 15 81 72

____ ____ ____ ____
32 72 16 63

____ ____ ____ ____
20 16 24 72

____ ____ ____ ____ ____ ."
15 81 12 72 49

(Matthew 18:35)

Directions

Jesus gave His disciples specific directions on how to pray. Write the letter that comes two letters after the letter given to discover how Jesus wanted His disciples to pray. Will you pray this way?

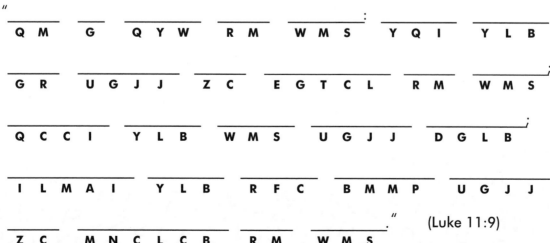

"____ ____ ____ ____ ____ ____ ____ ____ :
Q M   G   Q Y W   R M   W M S   Y Q I   Y L B

____ ____ ____ ____ ____ ;
G R   U G J J   Z C   E G T C L   R M   W M S

____ ____ ____ ____ ____ ;
Q C C I   Y L B   W M S   U G J J   D G L B

____ ____ ____ ____ ____ ____
I L M A I   Y L B   R F C   B M M P   U G J J

____ ____ ____ ____ ." (Luke 11:9)
Z C   M N C L C B   R M   W M S

Just One

How important is just one person? Missionaries sometimes work for years before seeing one person give his life to Christ. Jesus used the Parables of the Lost Sheep and Coin to show just how important each individual person is to Him.

Find the code for each letter by adding the numbers next to it. Then solve the puzzle.

A	$3 + 5 + 8 + 2 =$ ____
B	$6 + 2 + 5 + 1 =$ ____
C	$8 + 7 + 8 + 7 =$ ____
D	$6 + 2 + 5 + 8 =$ ____
E	$9 + 9 + 9 + 9 =$ ____
G	$4 + 5 + 1 + 5 =$ ____
H	$8 + 9 + 3 + 8 =$ ____
I	$5 + 4 + 6 + 5 =$ ____
J	$7 + 9 + 8 + 9 =$ ____
L	$2 + 1 + 3 + 4 =$ ____
M	$7 + 6 + 7 + 9 =$ ____
N	$5 + 2 + 3 + 2 =$ ____
O	$8 + 4 + 8 + 4 =$ ____
P	$9 + 3 + 6 + 9 =$ ____
R	$4 + 2 + 9 + 1 =$ ____
S	$7 + 7 + 7 + 2 =$ ____
T	$9 + 8 + 7 + 1 =$ ____
U	$3 + 2 + 4 + 2 =$ ____
V	$7 + 4 + 3 + 5 =$ ____
W	$7 + 6 + 5 + 4 =$ ____
Y	$9 + 8 + 9 + 8 =$ ____

"____ ____ ____ ____
20   25 36 10 10   34 24 11   25 28 18 25

____ ____ ____ ____
20 12   25 28 36   23 18 29 36   22 18 34

____ ____ ____
25 28 36 16 36   22 20 10 10   14 36

____ ____
29 24 16 36   16 36 33 24 20 30 20 12 15

____ ____ ____
20 12   28 36 18 19 36 12   24 19 36 16

____ ____ ____
24 12 36   23 20 12 12 36 16   22 28 24

____ ____
16 36 27 36 12 25 23   25 28 18 12

____ ____-
24 19 36 16   12 20 12 36 25 34

____ ____
12 20 12 36   16 20 15 28 25 36 24 11 23

____ ____
27 36 16 23 24 12 23   22 28 24

____ ____ ____
21 24   12 24 25   12 36 36 21

____ ____."
25 24   16 36 27 36 12 25

(Luke 15:7)

Special Words

Lazarus, the brother of Mary and Martha, had died. Jesus and His disciples arrived several days after Lazarus's death. What special words did Jesus use to raise Lazarus from the dead? Color all the boxes with "1" red. Color all the boxes with other numbers blue.

5	6	7	8	9	0	3	2	5	7	6	4	5	7	8	9	7	6	8	5	4	8	3	4	6	9	2	5	7
5	1	3	6	7	1	1	1	8	1	1	1	6	1	1	1	9	1	1	1	7	1	4	1	5	1	1	1	9
5	1	5	9	7	1	3	1	5	9	4	1	4	1	6	1	8	1	5	1	5	1	4	1	4	1	8	6	9
7	1	9	7	4	1	1	1	8	5	1	3	7	1	1	1	7	1	1	1	7	1	4	1	7	1	1	1	9
5	1	4	7	9	1	6	1	3	1	6	8	4	1	3	1	4	1	1	7	9	1	4	1	4	9	6	1	2
8	1	1	3	1	6	1	3	1	1	1	7	1	4	1	7	1	7	1	8	1	1	1	8	1	1	1	1	7
9	8	3	5	2	5	8	9	8	5	2	3	5	6	7	9	5	6	7	4	5	3	7	9	2	5	7	4	8
3	6	7	3	8	9	1	1	1	4	1	1	1	7	1	1	6	1	1	8	1	1	1	8	9	3	6	4	8
2	6	8	2	6	9	1	3	6	7	1	5	1	7	1	8	1	9	1	6	1	6	8	7	9	5	3	8	2
4	7	9	3	6	4	1	4	8	2	1	9	1	6	1	6	9	3	1	7	1	1	6	8	9	5	4	2	7
5	7	9	2	4	7	1	2	6	9	1	4	1	7	1	4	7	5	1	6	1	4	7	8	9	2	5	3	6
6	8	4	6	9	2	1	1	1	5	1	1	1	4	1	6	8	3	1	0	1	1	1	6	8	2	4	0	5
6	9	5	6	2	3	8	6	7	9	8	4	3	2	5	6	9	7	8	5	4	2	5	7	8	9	5	7	3
4	5	9	2	8	5	8	3	5	1	1	1	1	5	1	3	1	7	1	1	1	4	7	9	5	3	7	5	4	8
4	7	5	8	2	4	9	7	8	1	4	1	7	1	6	1	0	7	1	2	6	7	9	5	7	4	6	2	9
8	9	3	6	2	8	4	6	8	1	5	1	7	1	4	1	7	5	1	4	0	9	4	6	2	4	9	7	6
4	7	3	8	9	6	2	4	6	1	9	1	8	1	7	1	9	6	1	7	9	4	7	2	4	7	4	9	2
2	6	9	5	8	4	7	3	9	1	1	1	6	1	1	1	5	8	1	8	9	5	7	3	5	2	8	6	7
7	4	6	4	2	9	8	3	5	3	2	8	6	2	4	0	6	7	5	8	4	6	4	5	2	8	9	7	4

Blind Faith

A	B	C	D	E	F	G	H	I	J	K	L	M
72	38	43	56	99	67	19	26	31	92	51	48	79

N	O	P	Q	R	S	T	U	V	W	X	Y	Z
62	21	45	17	95	69	88	55	33	96	74	29	83

. . . .

Subtract 7 from each number.

. . . .

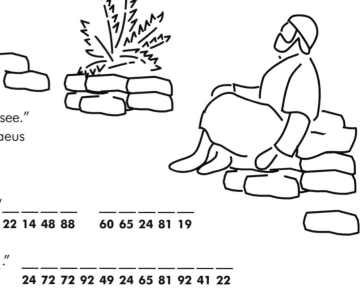

Blind Bartimaeus shouted to Jesus to have mercy on him. He was brought before Jesus and he asked, "Rabbi, I want to see." What special message did Jesus give Bartimaeus before restoring his sight?

" __ __ ,' __ __ __ __ __   __ __ __ __ __ ,' " __ __ __ __   __ __ __ __ __
  12 14   62 65 24 49   85 92 62 48 62   22 14 48 88   60 65 24 81 19

__ __ __   __ __ __ __ __ __   __ __ __ . " __ __ __ __ __ __ __ __ __ __ __ __ __
19 65 62   19 92 65 41 92 49   22 14 48   24 72 72 92 49 24 65 81 92 41 22

__ __   __ __ __ __ __ __ __ __   __ __ __   __ __ __ __ __   __ __ __
19 92   88 92 36 92 24 26 92 49   19 24 62   62 24 12 19 81   65 55 49

__ __ __ __ __ __ __ __   __ __ __ __ __   __ __ __ __ __   __ __ __ __ __ __ .
60 14 41 41 14 89 92 49   85 92 62 48 62   65 41 14 55 12   81 19 92   88 14 65 49

(Mark 10:52)

The Greatest One

Jesus was asked to select the greatest commandment in the law. Write the letter that comes two letters before the letter given to discover Jesus' answer. Think of different ways you can follow this commandment.

_____ _____ :
L G U W U   T G R N K G F

" ____ ____ ____ ____ ___
   N Q X G   V J G   N Q T F   A Q W T   I Q F

____ ___ ____ _____
Y K V J   C N N   A Q W T   J G C T V

___ ____ ___ ____ ____
C P F   Y K V J   C N N   A Q W T   U Q W N

___ ____ ___ ____ ____ '
C P F   Y K V J   C N N   A Q W T   O K P F

____ __ ___ _____ ___
V J K U   K U   V J G   H K T U V   C P F

_____ _____ "
I T G C V G U V   E Q O O C P F O G P V

(Matthew 22:37, 38)

He Will Return

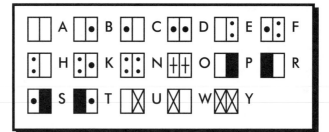

Use the flag code in the box to figure out the message.

Jesus promised that He would return for us some day. He told us to be prepared for His second coming. But when is that wonderful day going to happen?

"

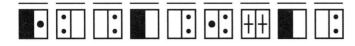

(Matthew 25:13)

Talents

God has given all of us various degrees of talent. What does He expect us to do with these wonderful gifts? Finish each word with its correct ending to find out.

AS
ACE
HERS
SE
D'S
TS
NE
IOUS
N
FT
RVE
RMS
EIVED
EVER
FULLY
ULD
E
TERING
CH
O

EA _____   O _____

SHO _____

U _____

WHAT _____   GI _____

H ___   H _____   REC _____

T ___   SE _____   OT _____ ,

FAITH _____

ADMINIS _____

GO _____   GR _____   I ___

I _____   VAR _____   FO _____ .

(1 Peter 4:10)

What a Meal!

Jesus was eating the Passover meal on the night before He died. At this time He instituted a special meal called the Lord's Supper. Decipher the code below to find out what special ingredients are included in this meal and what each one represents.

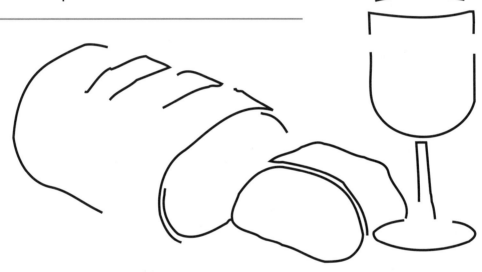

A=26, E=22, I=18, O=12, U=6

```
 __  __  __     __  __  __  __  __ ,   __  __  __  __  __
 07  19  22     25  09  22  26  23     04  19  18  24  19

 __  __  __  __  __  __  __  __  __  __     __  __  __     __  __  __  __ .
 09  22  11  09  22  08  22  13  07  08     19  18  08     25  12  23  02

 __  __  __     __  __  __ ,   __  __  __  __  __
 07  19  22     24  06  11     04  19  18  24  19

 __  __  __  __  __  __  __  __  __  __     __  __  __     __  __  __  __  __ .
 09  22  11  09  22  08  22  13  07  08     19  18  08     25  15  12  12  23
```

Humiliated Vowels

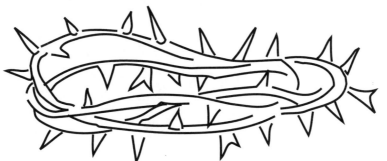

Mark 15:16-20 describes a scene that happened before Jesus was crucified. The description is written below but the vowels are so humiliated by what happened that they have switched places. To correct the vowels, use the key provided.

A = E
E = I
I = O
O = U
U = A

After _____ was _____ and taken _____ , He was led
      JASOS   **URRASTAD**   **UWUY**

to the _____ where the _____ _____ Him.
      PULUCA   **SILDEARS**   **MICKAD**

They _____ Him in a _____ robe and placed a _____ of
      DRASSAD   **PORPLA**   **CRIWN**

_____ _____ on His _____ . They _____ Him the
  TWESTAD   **THIRNS**   **HAUD**   **CULLAD**

_____ of the _____ , _____ Him on the _____ with a _____ ,
 KENG   **JAWS**   **STROCK**   **HAUD**   **STUFF**

and then _____ on Him. When they _____ , they put His
      SPET   **FENESHAD**

_____ back on Him and _____ Him away to be _____ .
  CLITHAS   **LAD**   **CROCEFEAD**

The Women and the Angel

Find the answer to the puzzle by comparing the individual stones with the wall of stones. When a match is found, transfer the letters to the large stones. Then write the letters on the lines provided.

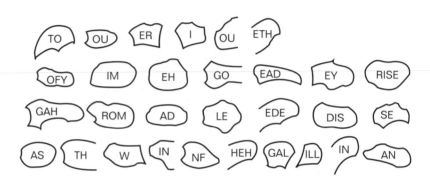

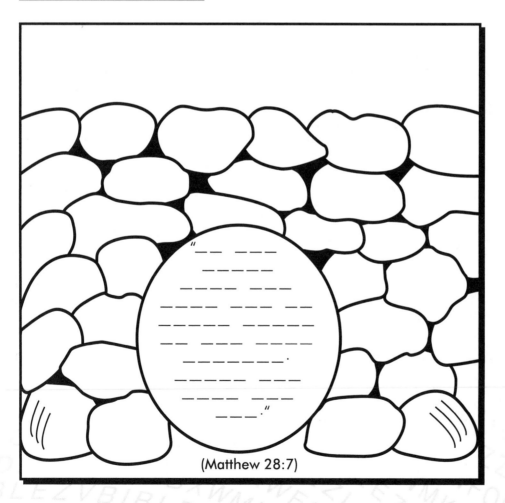

(Matthew 28:7)

Mary Magdalene and the other Mary went to look at Jesus' tomb. There was a violent earthquake. An angel came to the tomb, rolled back the stone, and sat on it. The soldiers guarding the tomb fainted. The angel told the women not to be frightened because Jesus was alive! What were the women told to tell Jesus' disciples? Solve the puzzle to find the answer.

Thomas's Unbelief

John 20:10-31 gives details of Jesus' appearance to His disciples after His death. Thomas wasn't present the first time Jesus appeared, and Thomas declared that he wouldn't believe unless he had touched Jesus' wounds. Finally Thomas saw and touched Jesus. What did Jesus tell him?

On the lines below rewrite the message using the letters in the box. Begin with the last letter and work backwards. The first and last letters have already been entered. False punctuation has been included in order to make the solution harder to find.

" B ___ ___ ___ ___ ___ ___ ',

___ ___ ___ ___ ; ___ ___

___ ___ ___ ___ ___ ___

___ ___ ___ ___ ___ ___ D ."

```
D E V E I L E ! B E V A H
, T E Y D N A " N E E S
T " O N E V A H . O H
! W E S O H T E R A , D
E S S E L . B D E V E I L
, E B E V A H , U O Y E
M . N E E S E V A H ; U
O Y , E S U , A C E B .
```

(John 20:29)

The Road to Emmaus
—Luke 24

On the Road to Emmaus

Cleopas and a companion were walking along the road to Emmaus when Jesus joined them. They didn't recognize Him until He revealed himself after the evening meal. Then He disappeared. What was the men's comment afterwards?

The path of circles below will lead you to the answer. Follow the correct path to the end and record all the letters in the spaces provided.

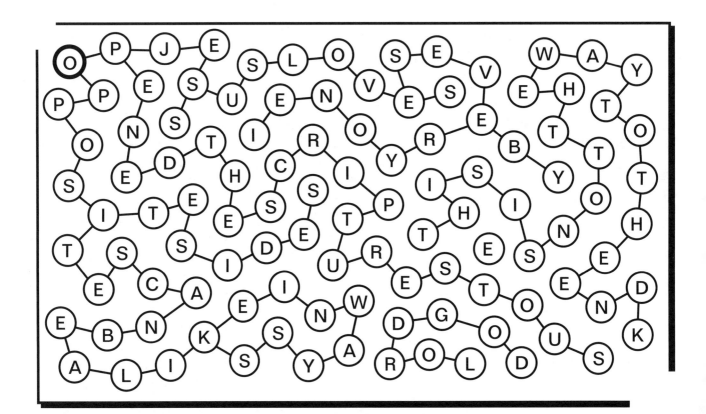

"Were not our hearts burning within us while he talked with us on the road and

_ _ _ _ _ _ _   _ _ _   _ _ _ _ _ _ _ _ _ _ _   _ _   _ _?"

(Luke 24:32)

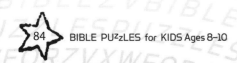

Jesus' Farewell

Cross out all 26 letters of the alphabet in order. (Begin at the bottom.) Write the remaining letters on the lines provided.

STOPTHEQVRESTRYUENDVOFWTXHEYAGZE

NYOSMANYWWALUO

WITHKYIYIAJHGFLEERUDCSBA

What was the last thing Jesus said to the disciples before He went into Heaven?

" _ _ _ _ _   _   _ _   _ _ _   _ _ _   _ _ _ _ _,'

_ _   _ _ _   _ _ _   _ _   _ _ _   _ _ _."

(Matthew 28:20)

Peter Preaches Salvation

To solve this puzzle-graph, begin with row #1 and move down the column to the first dot. Write the letter from the left-hand column on the blank below. Continue down the row to the next dot or proceed to the next column if no dots are found.

Peter preached to a huge crowd on the day of Pentecost. When the people asked him what they should do, what did Peter say?

" __ __ __ __ __ __

__ __ __

__ __ __

__ __ __ __ __ __ __ __ __ __ __ __."

(Acts 2:38)

	1	2	3	4	5	6	7	8	9	10	11	12	13	14	15
A					•					•					
B							•		•						
C															
D						•									•
E		•	•				•							•	
F															
G															
H															
I												•			
J															
K															
L															
M															
N			•		•										
O															
P		•							•						
Q															
R	•														
S															
T				•							•				
U															
V															
W															
X															
Y															
Z													•		

A Crippled Beggar

What did Peter say to the crippled beggar?

The answer is hidden below. All the letters are present but they have been arranged with extra spaces between them. Study the letters. Write the complete words on the lines provided.

SI   LVER   ORG   OLD   ID   ONO   THAVE   BU   TWHA

TIH   AVE   IGI   VE   YO   UIN   TH   ENA   MEOF   JES

USCH   RIS   TOF   NA   ZAR   ETH   WA   LK

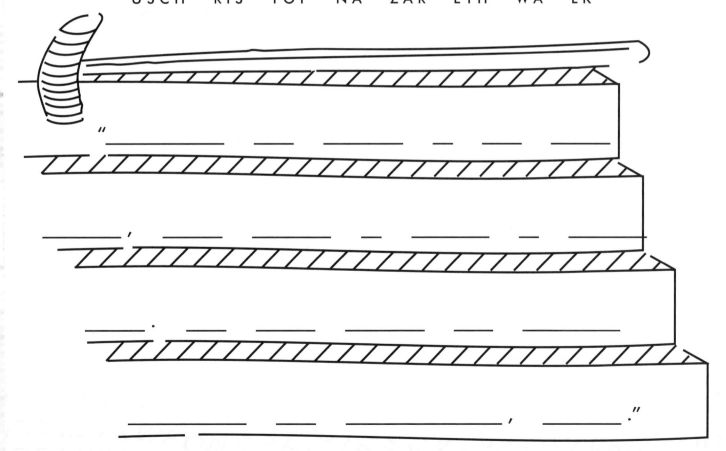

(Acts 3:6)

Peter Speaks Up

Use the graph to decode the message. Each letter is represented by two numbers. The first number is for the vertical row and the second is for the horizontal row. Follow each row until you come to the letter. Example: 42=M.

	1	2	3	4	5
1	F	S	H	N	B
2	Y	O	A	L	U
3	C	I	R	X	G
4	T	M	W	D	P
5	J	E	Q	K	V

What was Peter's reply to the Sanhedrin?

"___ ___ ___ ___ ___ ___ ___ ___ ___   ___ ___   ___ ___ ___ ___ ___   ___ ___   ___ ___   ___ ___ ___
12 23 24 55 23 41 32 22 14   32 12   11 22 25 14 44   32 14   14 22   22 14 52

___ ___ ___ ___,   ___ ___ ___   ___ ___ ___ ___ ___   ___ ___   ___ ___ ___ ___ ___
52 24 12 52   11 22 33   41 13 52 33 52   32 12   14 22   22 41 13 52 33

___ ___ ___ ___   ___ ___ ___ ___ ___   ___ ___ ___ ___ ___ ___   ___ ___ ___ ___ ___   ___ ___
14 23 42 52   25 14 44 52 33   13 52 23 55 52 14   35 32 55 52 14   41 22

___ ___ ___   ___ ___   ___ ___ ___ ___ ___   ___ ___   ___ ___ ___ ___   ___ ___   ___ ___ ___ ___ ___ ___."
42 52 14   15 21   43 13 32 31 13   43 52   42 25 12 41   15 52   12 23 55 52 44

(Acts 4:12)

A Vision

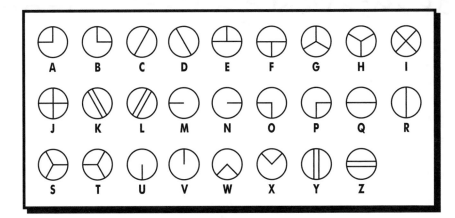

Use the code
to interpret
the message.

Stephen stood before the Sanhedrin and accused them of being like their fathers—
killing the prophets and the Righteous One. They became furious, but what did
Stephen say that finally caused them to drag him outside and stone him?

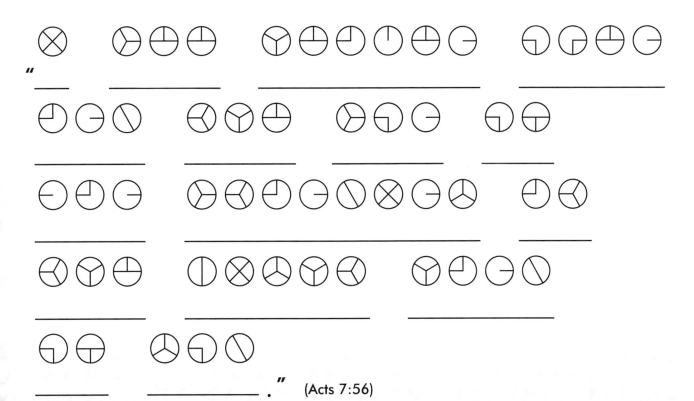

." (Acts 7:56)

Philip's Journey

An angel told Philip to go south to the desert road from Jerusalem to Gaza. Along the way he joined an Ethiopian man who was reading from the book of Isaiah. The Ethiopian invited Philip into his chariot and Philip explained the Scriptures to him. What did the man ask Philip when they saw some water?

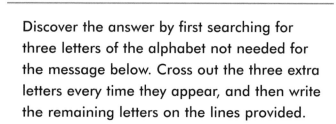

Discover the answer by first searching for three letters of the alphabet not needed for the message below. Cross out the three extra letters every time they appear, and then write the remaining letters on the lines provided.

C L C O O K H E M R E G I S W C A T G E R W C H M Y S
H O U G L C D N C T I M B E M B A G P C T I C Z M E D

" _ _ _ _ , _ _ _ _ _ _ _ _ _ _ _ . _ _ _

_ _ _ _ _ _ _ ' _ _ _ _ _ _ _ _ _ _ _ _ ? "

(Acts 8:36)

A Visit with the Enemy

To solve the puzzle, transfer all the letters in the boxes with a △ in the corner to the lines provided.

O E	O N	△ G	△ O	△ T	O O	O G	△ H	△ I	O G	O H	O U
△ S	O I	O T	△ M	△ A	O M	△ N	O E	O K	△ I	△ S	O T
O I	△ M	O Y	O N	△ Y	△ C	O O	△ H	O A	O R	△ O	O C
△ S	△ E	△ N	O T	O H	△ I	△ N	O O	O N	△ S	△ T	O I
O H	O E	△ R	△ U	O N	△ M	O N	△ E	△ N	O E	O A	△ T

Saul was struck blind on his way to Damascus, and Jesus spoke with him. For three days Saul stayed in Damascus, fasted, and prayed. The Lord instructed Ananias to go to Saul, but Ananias was afraid. What was the Lord's response to Ananias's fear?

" _ _ ! _ _ _ _   _ _ _

_ _ _ _ _ _ _ _ _ _

_ _ _ _ _ _ _ _ _ . "

(Acts 9:15)

Peter Raises Dorcas

—Acts 9

A Miraculous Recovery

Use the diagram to decipher the code.

In Joppa there was a disciple named Dorcas who was always doing good and helping the poor. She became sick and died. Her body was washed and placed in an upstairs room. Two men were sent to Peter and they urged him to return with them. When Peter arrived, all the widows wept and showed him the robes and clothes Dorcas had made for them. What did Peter do next?

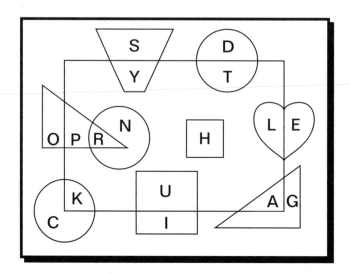

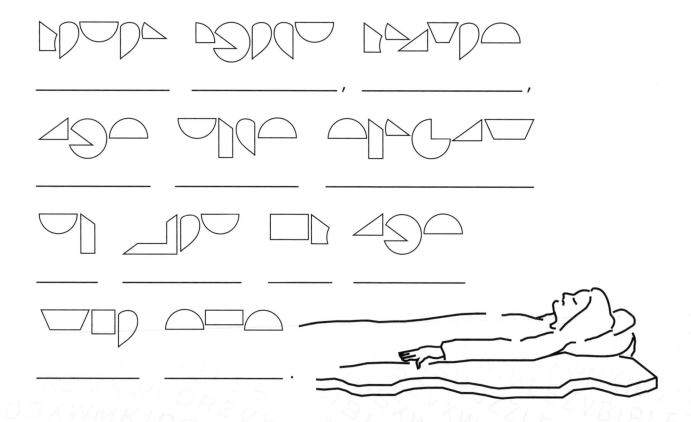

Switching Sides

To find the answer, switch the first two letters of all words that contain three or four letters. For all words with five or more letters, switch the first two and last two letters.

God instructed Peter to go to Cornelius's home, but Peter was reluctant to go. Peter had an important revelation after he got there. What was it?

_____ _____:

E P T R E   A S I D

" __ ___ _____ ___

I   O N W   E R A L I E Z   O H W

____ __ __ ____ ___ ____ ___

R T U E   I T   I S   H T A T   O G D   O D E S   O N T

____ _____ ___ _____

H S O W   A F V O R I T I M S   U B T   C A C E P S T

___ ____ ____ _____ ___ ____

E M N   R F O M   V E E Y R   A N T I N O   H W O   E F A R

___ ___ __ ____ __ _____."

I H M   N A D   D O   H W A T   I S   I R G T H

(Acts 10:34)

Four Times Four

King Herod arrested Peter and ordered four squads of four soldiers each to guard him in prison. The church prayed earnestly for Peter, and God answered. What was Peter's response when he reached the streets?

Find the answer by using the code in the box.

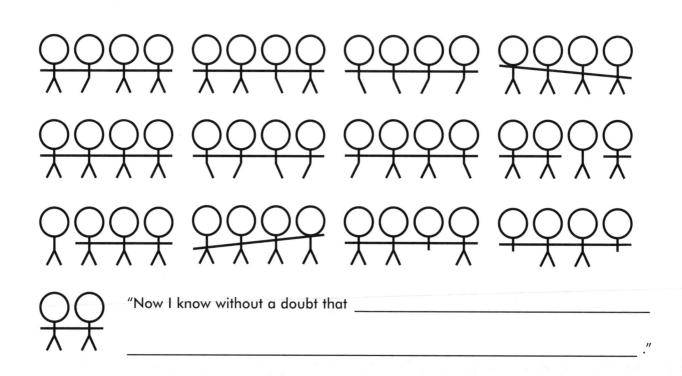

"Now I know without a doubt that _____

_____."

(Acts 12:11)

Are We Gods?

The citizens of Lystra thought that Paul and Barnabas were gods in human form. They brought bulls and wreaths and wanted to offer sacrifices to them. But what message did Paul and Barnabas shout to them?

Follow the instructions in order to discover the answer.
Change the letter B to E.
Change the letter F to O.
Change the letter P to M.
Change the letter C to I.
Change the letter V to A.
Change the letter Z to Y.
Leave all other letters the same.

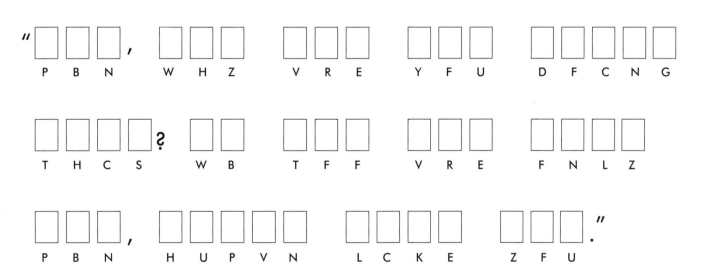

"☐☐☐, ☐☐☐ ☐☐☐ ☐☐☐ ☐☐☐☐☐
 P B N   W H Z   V R E   Y F U   D F C N G

☐☐☐☐? ☐☐ ☐☐☐ ☐☐☐ ☐☐☐☐
 T H C S   W B   T F F   V R E   F N L Z

☐☐☐, ☐☐☐☐☐ ☐☐☐☐ ☐☐☐."
 P B N   H U P V N   L C K E   Z F U

(Acts 14:15)

Lydia's Conversion
—Acts 16

A Message for Lydia

Paul and Silas spoke to a group of women beside a river near Philippi. One of the women was Lydia, a dealer of purple cloth. How did she respond to Paul's message?

To answer the question, first follow the directions for numbers 1–11. Then transfer the answers to the matching numbered lines to complete the message.

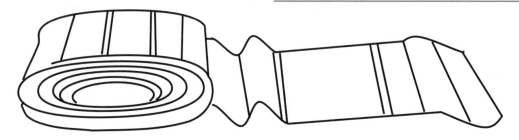

The _____ _____ her
6   5

_____ to _____
11   7

to _____ _____ ....
8   2

_____ and the _____
1   4

of _____ _____
10   9

were _____ .
3

1. another name for "her"
2. a communication in writing or speech
3. means "immersed"
4. part of a church
5. opposite of closed
6. another name for God
7. to say something in return
8. the last apostle (add 's)
9. those who live under one roof
10. another name for "she"
11. symbol for love

(Acts 16:14, 15)

No Prison Can Hold Them

1. you chew with these _____
   10 5 35 9 36

2. another name for prison _____
   13 3 15 38

3. another name for TV _____
   27 12 16 47 46 23 34 28 32 26

4. your fingers are attached to it _____
   22 1 20 39

5. opposite of north _____
   44 17 33 55 31

6. another name for shade _____
   6 11 19 21 37 40

7. something you do when you sleep _____
   48 18 25 14 50

8. reddish brittle coating on iron _____
   42 7 2 51

9. another word for screech _____
   24 52 29 43 45 52

10. fishing line is wound on it _____
    4 41 30 8

While in Philippi, Paul and Silas were arrested, beaten, and thrown in prison. Instead of moaning and groaning about their situation, they prayed and sang hymns to God. Suddenly there was a violent earthquake that shook the foundations of the prison. The prison doors flew open but none of the prisoners escaped. What was the jailor's reaction to this miracle?

Fill in the answers to the questions in the box. Then use the numbered letters to solve the puzzle.

__ __
1 2   3   4 5 6 7 8 9   10 11 12   13 14 15 16 17 18   19 20 21   22 23 24

__ .
25 26 27 28 29 30   31 32 33 34 35 36 37 38 39   40 41 42 43   44 45 46 47 48

While He Was Speaking

The apostle Paul met with believers in Troas for fellowship and teaching. One night, while Paul was speaking, a young man fell out of a window and died.

"Paul went down, threw himself on the young man and put his arms around him. 'Don't be alarmed,' he said. 'He's alive!'" (Acts 20:10)

All the words from Acts 20:10 are hidden in the puzzle. Find and circle the words. Then copy the remaining letters, except the letter X, in order on the blanks provided. You will learn the name of the young man who was restored to life. Read Acts 20:9 to check your answer.

T	H	H	X	D	X	A	L	I	V	E	A	P	T	X
H	I	I	X	O	X	L	X	X	X	X	N	A	H	X
R	M	S	E	W	X	A	R	O	U	N	D	U	E	Y
E	S	U	X	N	A	R	M	S	N	H	T	L	W	O
W	E	Y	H	I	M	M	P	M	X	E	C	X	E	U
X	L	B	E	X	H	E	U	X	A	S	X	H	N	N
X	F	U	S	A	I	D	T	D	O	N	T	S	T	G

What was the young man's name? _ _ _ _ _ _ _

Who Says?

Read about the plot to kill Paul in Acts 23:1-12, 16-24, 31. Who said or who might have said these things? Put your answers on the spaces provided. Then use the numbered letters to solve the puzzle in the box.

Paul said,
"I am a ___ ___ ___ ___ ___ ___ ___ ___.
            1 2 3 4 5 6 7 8
I stand on trial because of my hope in the resurrection of the dead."

"Strike Paul on the mouth!"   ___ ___ ___ ___ ___ ___ ___
                                          5

"I did not realize that he was the high priest."   ___ ___ ___ ___
                                                         1

"There is no resurrection!"   ___ ___ ___ ___ ___ ___ ___ ___ ___
                                        3

"I'm afraid for Paul. Take him to the barracks."   ___ ___ ___ ___ ___ ___ ___ ___ ___
                                                                              4

"You must testify about me in Rome."   ___ ___ ___ ___ ___ ___ ___
                                                  7

"We will not eat or drink until we kill Paul."   ___ ___ ___ ___ ___ ___ ___ ___
                                                                       6

"More than forty men are waiting to kill Paul."   ___ ___ ___ ___ ___ ___

                                                   ___ ___ ___ ___ ___ ___
                                                              2

"Paul asked me to bring this young man to you because he has something to tell you."   ___ ___ ___ ___ ___ ___ ___ ___
                                                                                                  8

Safe from the Storms

Paul was on a ship sailing for Rome when a terrible storm hit. Find your way through the maze to find out what happened to Paul.

Begin

Rome!

GOD KEPT PAUL SAFE SO HE COULD PREACH ABOUT THE KINGDOM OF GOD AND TEACH ABOUT JESUS

PAUL AND ALL HIS COMPANIONS WERE KILLED IN THE STORM

God's Gift

Use the code to learn about a wonderful gift that God offers to every person. After you have filled in the coded letters, use the vowel list to help you decide where each vowel should go. Read Romans 6:23 to check your answer.

Vowels

A E E E
E E I I
I I I O
O O O
U U

Be Good!
—Romans 12;
Galatians 6

Guides for Life

Read each of these sentences. If the sentence is true, circle the letter under True. If it is false, circle the letter under False. Read Romans 12:9-21 to check your answer.

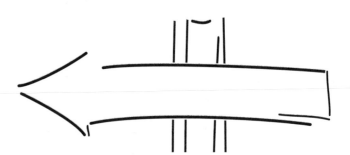

The Bible sometimes gives us lists of things we should and should not do. One of those lists is found in Romans 12:9-21.

		True	False
1.	Honor yourself above others.	K	P
2.	Be faithful in prayer.	E	A
3.	Do not share with people who are in need.	U	O
4.	Curse those who persecute you.	N	P
5.	Live at peace with everyone.	L	F
6.	Overcome evil with good.	E	I

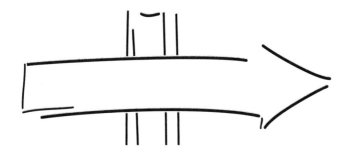

Copy the letters you circled, in order, onto the blanks below to finish this quote from Galatians 6:10.

Therefore, as we have opportunity,

let us do good to all __ __ __ __ __ __ ,

especially to those who belong to the family of believers.

Fruit of the Spirit Scramble

Galatians 5:22, 23 lists the fruit of the Spirit, nine characteristics of people whose lives are influenced by the Holy Spirit. See if you can unscramble the words to list the fruit of the Spirit. How are you showing the fruit of the Spirit in your life?

_ _ _ _

_ _ _

_ _ _ _ _

_ _ _ _ _ _ _ _

_ _ _ _ _ _ _ _

_ _ _ _ _ _ _ _

_ _ _ _ _ _ _ _ _ _

_ _ _ _ _ _ _ _ _ _ _

_ _ _ _ _ - _ _ _ _ _ _

In the Lord's Army

The book of Ephesians tells about six pieces of the armor of God. First, write the letter that comes two letters before each letter on the lines to find a description of what each piece of armor represents. (Example: A=Y.) Then draw a line from each description to the piece of armor it represents. Read Ephesians 6:14-17 to check your answers.

1. __ __ __ __ __
V   T   W   V   J

2. __ __ __ __ __ __ __ __ **that comes from the**
T   G   C   F   K   P   G   U   U

__ __ __ __ __ __ **of peace**
I   Q   U   R   G   N

3. __ __ __ __ __ __ __ __
U   C   N   X   C   V   K   Q   P

4. __ __ __ __   __ __   __ __ __
Y   Q   T   F   Q   H   I   Q   F

5. __ __ __ __ __ __ __ __ __ __ __
T   K   I   J   V   G   Q   W   U   P   G   U   U

6. __ __ __ __ __
H   C   K   V   J

Use God's armor so you can be strong in the Lord and in His mighty power!

Standing Firm

—Philippians 1, 2, 4

Words for the Wise

Find and read the Scriptures to solve this puzzle. How do you stand firm in the Lord? (Read Philippians 1:27.)

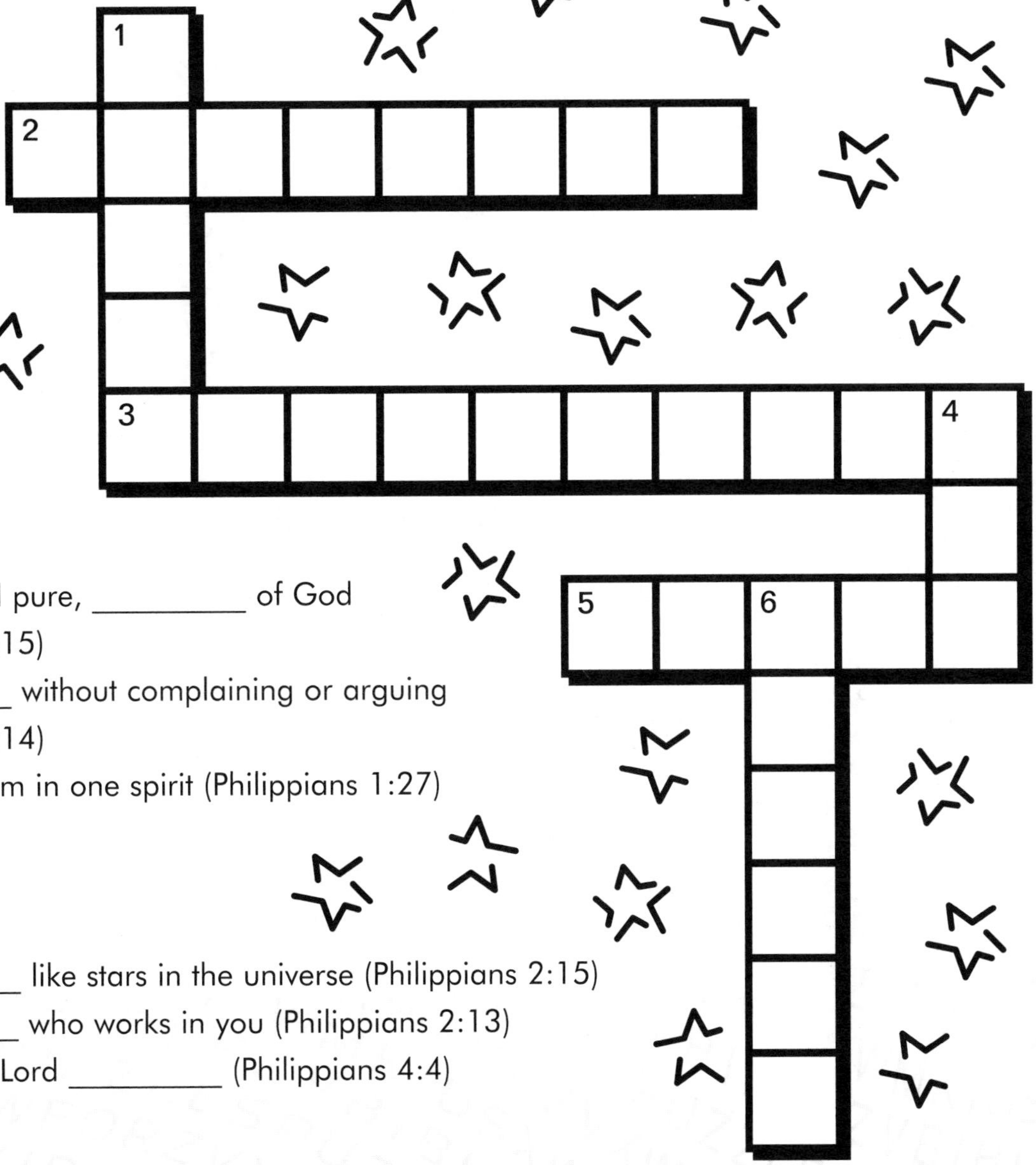

ACROSS

2 blameless and pure, _________ of God (Philippians 2:15)

3 Do _________ without complaining or arguing (Philippians 2:14)

5 _________ firm in one spirit (Philippians 1:27)

DOWN

1 you _________ like stars in the universe (Philippians 2:15)

4 it is _________ who works in you (Philippians 2:13)

6 Rejoice in the Lord _________ (Philippians 4:4)

Instructions on Christian Living
—1 Thessalonians 3–5

The Good Life

God gives us instructions in the Bible for how to live our lives happily. Follow the instructions below to learn three things God wants us to do. Read 1 Thessalonians 5:16-18 to check your answer.

Cross out all words ending in *ing*.
Cross out all girls' names.
Cross out all shapes.
Cross out all words that rhyme with *heart*.

Be enjoying Renee joyful circle always; running pray start Beth continually; cart give square thanks loving in all dart praying circumstances, for this diamond Jill is God's loving will giving triangle for Amy you in art Christ Jesus.

Way to Grow!

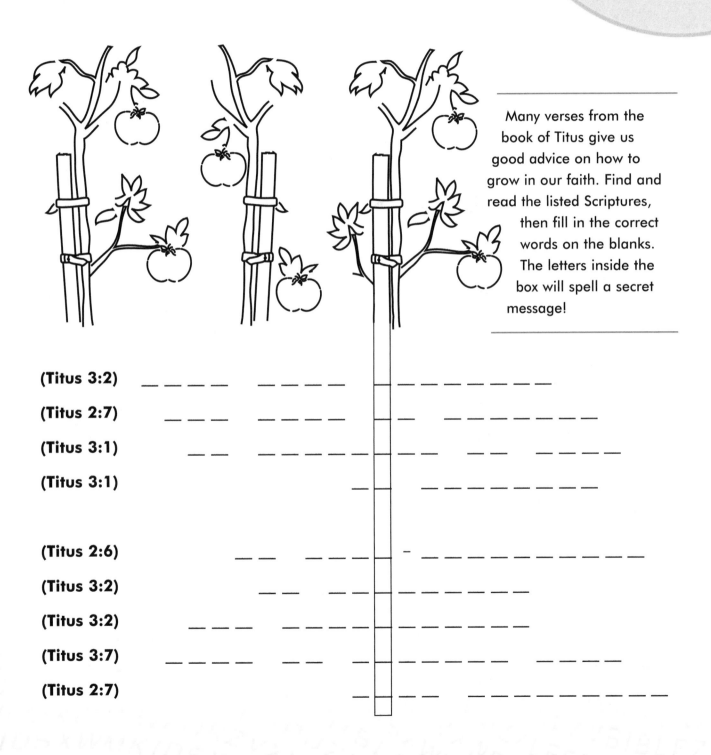

Many verses from the book of Titus give us good advice on how to grow in our faith. Find and read the listed Scriptures, then fill in the correct words on the blanks. The letters inside the box will spell a secret message!

(Titus 3:2) _ _ _ _ _   _ _ _ _   _ _ _ _ _ _ _ _ _

(Titus 2:7) _ _ _   _ _ _ _   _ _ _ _ _ _

(Titus 3:1) _ _   _ _ _ _ _ _ _ _ _   _ _ _ _ _ _ _

(Titus 3:1) _   _ _ _ _ _ _ _ _

(Titus 2:6) _ _   _ _ _ _ _   _   _ _ _ _ _ _ _ _

(Titus 3:2) _ _   _ _ _ _ _ _ _ _

(Titus 3:2) _ _ _   _ _ _ _ _ _ _

(Titus 3:7) _ _ _ _   _ _ _   _ _ _ _ _

(Titus 2:7) _ _ _ _   _ _ _ _ _ _ _ _

True Wisdom
—James 1–4

Be Wise

Solve this picture puzzle to learn how to get true wisdom. Read James 4:8 to check your answer.

 − **N** + **M** = _____

N + = _____

2 = _____

 + **D** = _____

& = _____

 − **S E P** = _____

 − **E** + **I** = _____

 − **N** + **M** = _____

N + = _____

2 = _____

 U = _____

True Love

Look at the different heart shapes on this page. There are six different shapes, and each of those six have one that looks just like it. Draw lines to connect each heart shape to its match. Then read what the heart shapes tell about love. Read 1 John 4:7-21 to check your answers.

because he first loved us.

Dear friends, let

in God, and God in him.

also ought to love one another.

God, but that he loved us.

must also love his brother.

us love one another.

We love

Since God so loved us, we

Whoever loves God

This is love: not that we loved

Whoever lives in love lives

Heavenly Praise

The last book of the Bible tells how God is praised in Heaven. In the puzzle below, 15 words relating to the praise of God are hidden. See if you can find them all!

angel
blessed
glory
God
hear
honor
Jesus
language
people
power
praise
strength
thanks
throne
wisdom

B W M J B H E A R H Q D T
P I O A L O N G L N O E H
G S V C E F P R A I S E A
T D U K S T R E N G T H N
H O J E S U S R G R Y L K
R M B S E A N E U T J D S
O X G O D R L W A N G E L
N E W N K I Z O G L O R Y
E H O N O R C P E O P L E

Heavenly Hunt

The book of Revelation tells us about Jesus and God and Heaven. Draw lines to match the beginnings of these sentences with their proper endings. Be careful! The shapes do not match! Find and read the Scriptures to check your answers.

"I am the Alpha

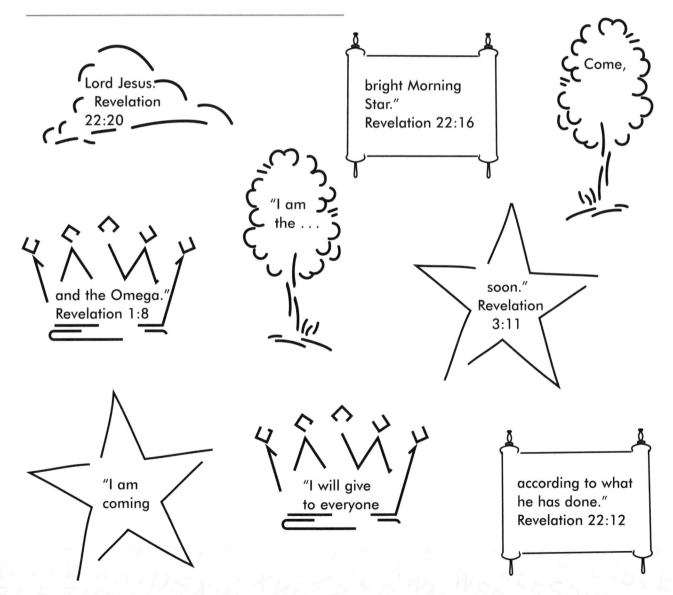

Lord Jesus. Revelation 22:20

bright Morning Star." Revelation 22:16

Come,

"I am the . . .

and the Omega." Revelation 1:8

soon." Revelation 3:11

"I am coming

"I will give to everyone

according to what he has done." Revelation 22:12

Forever Praising

God is the only one who deserves our praise. We can praise Him now and we will praise Him in Heaven. The words in the cloud shape come from the book of Revelation. They tell reasons why we should praise God. Fit the words into the acrostic puzzle below. How will you praise God today?

great
marvelous
almighty
true
king
holy
righteous
salvation
power

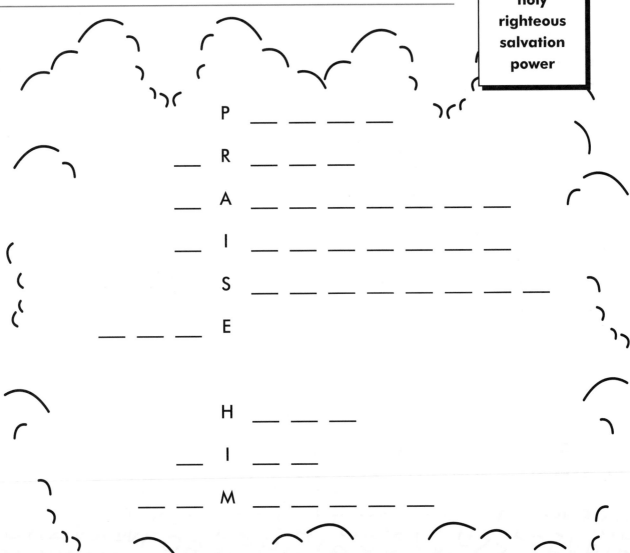

P _ _ _ _

_ R _ _ _

_ A _ _ _ _ _ _

_ I _ _ _ _ _ _

S _ _ _ _ _ _ _

_ _ _ _ E

H _ _ _

_ I _ _

_ _ _ M _ _

Genesis 1:1

When two letters go walking, only one does the talking. Discover the correct
word by choosing only one letter from each pair to fill in the blanks.

$\underline{UI}$ $\underline{NY}$　$\underline{TH}$ $\underline{HZ}$ $\underline{UE}$　$\underline{KB}$ $\underline{EA}$ $\underline{GM}$ $\underline{IO}$ $\underline{NR}$ $\underline{LN}$ $\underline{OI}$ $\underline{NX}$ $\underline{VG}$

$\underline{GK}$ $\underline{OE}$ $\underline{MD}$　$\underline{CV}$ $\underline{RD}$ $\underline{IE}$ $\underline{EA}$ $\underline{WT}$ $\underline{UE}$ $\underline{TD}$

$\underline{CT}$ $\underline{WH}$ $\underline{EA}$　$\underline{TH}$ $\underline{EI}$ $\underline{OA}$ $\underline{VT}$ $\underline{UE}$ $\underline{DN}$ $\underline{SC}$

$\underline{OA}$ $\underline{NK}$ $\underline{DW}$　$\underline{TV}$ $\underline{HY}$ $\underline{EU}$　$\underline{AE}$ $\underline{EA}$ $\underline{RC}$ $\underline{TD}$ $\underline{CH}$.

$\underline{GW}$ $\underline{EI}$ $\underline{SN}$ $\underline{IE}$ $\underline{SV}$ $\underline{EI}$ $\underline{KS}$ 1:1

Genesis 18:18

Discover the hidden verse! In the message below, some of the letters are filled in. Solve the code and solve the puzzle. Memorize the special promise God made.

```
        H
"  _ _ _ _ _ _    _ _ _    _ _ _ _ _
   Z Y I Z S Z N  D R O O  H F I V O B

                   G
   _ _ _ _ _ _  _  _ _ _ _ _  _ _ _
   Y V X L N V  Z  T I V Z G  Z M W

   _ _ _ _ _ _ _    _ _ _ _ _ _ '  _ _ _
   K L D V I U F O  M Z G R L M    Z M W

                                     H
   _ _ _    _ _ _ _ _ _ _ _    _ _    _ _ _ _ _
   Z O O    M Z G R L M H      L M    V Z I G S

   _ _ _ _    _ _    _ _ _ _ _ _ _
   D R O O    Y V    Y O V H H V W

    _ H _ _ _ G H    H _ _ ."
    G S I L F T S    S R N
```

A	B	C	D	E	F	G	H	I	J	K	L	M	N	O	P	Q	R	S	T	U	V	W	X	Y	Z

Exodus 15:11

Find and circle the words in the puzzle grid. Words can be found going any direction — up, down, diagonally or backwards. Words connected with a hyphen, such as THE-GODS, are found as one word.

Spell out the missing words with the leftover letters. Can you fill in the missing words before you find them? After you complete the challenges, practice reciting the verse.

Memory Verse

_ - _ - _   AMONG   THE-GODS

_ - _   _ - _ - _ - _   YOU-O

LORD?   WHO-IS   LIKE-YOU—

MAJESTIC   _ - _   HOLINESS,

AWESOME   IN-GLORY,

WORKING   WONDERS?   _ - _

- _ - _ - _ - _   15:11

Word Search

```
W H O W I O M S
L I I O K U A E
E S N R I O J M
T I G K G Y E O
H O L I N E S S
E H O N O K T E
G W R G M I I W
O N Y E A L C A
D R O L X O D U
S R E D N O W S
```

Deuteronomy 6:5

Decode each word by replacing each letter with one before or after it in the alphabet.
Replace A with Z or B, replace B with A or C, and so on. The words spell out the
Bible Memory verse. Rearrange the letters in the boxes to fill in the blanks below.

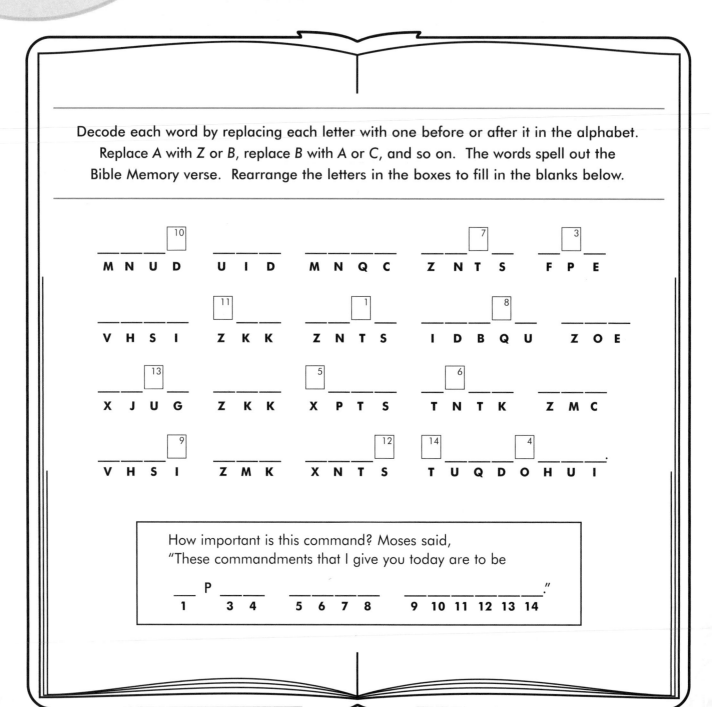

_ _ _ _ [10]   _ _ _   _ _ _ _   _ _ _ [7] _   _ _ [3] _

M N U D   U I D   M N Q C   Z N T S   F P E

_ _ _ [11] _   _ [1] _ _   _ _ _ [8] _   _ _ _

V H S I   Z K K   I D B Q U   Z O E

_ _ _ [13] _   _ [5] _   _ [6] _ _   _ _ _

X J U G   Z K K   T N T K   Z M C

_ _ _ [9] _   _ _ [12] _   [14] _ _ _ _ [4] _ .

V H S I   Z M K   X N T S   T U Q D O H U I

How important is this command? Moses said,
"These commandments that I give you today are to be

__ P ___ _____ _____."
 1   3 4   5 6 7 8   9 10 11 12 13 14

Joshua 1:9

Find and circle the words in the puzzle grid. Words can be found going any direction up, down, diagonally, or backwards. Words connected with a hyphen, such as I-NOT, are found as one word.

Spell out the missing words with the leftover letters. Can you fill in the missing words before you find them? After you complete the challenges, practice reciting the verse.

Memory Verse

"HAVE I-NOT COMMANDED

YOU-BE STRONG-AND __-__-__

-__-__-__-__-__-__ .

__-__- __-__-__ __-__

TERRIFIED; DO-NOT-BE __-__-__

-__-__-__-__-__-__-__ , FOR-THE

LORD YOUR-GOD WILL-BE

WITH-YOU WHEREVER YOU-

GO." JOSHUA (1:9)

Word Search

```
S C O F O R T H E U
R T J A G G E O U D
D R R O S D U C R W
O E W O S O T O N I
N V I N N H L M Y L
O E T F O G U M H L
T R H T I B A A E B
B E Y D I R V N S E
E H O C O E R D D U
R W U Y O U B E A G
E Y O U R G O D T D
```

2 Chronicles 7:14

Fit each of the words into the puzzle below. (Hint: Start with the longest word.) Words connected with a hyphen, such as IF-MY, are placed as one word. Words used more than once in the verse are included only once in the puzzle. Letters in the numbered squares answer the question below the puzzle. Three of the words have been placed for you.

Bible Memory Verse

IF-MY   PEOPLE,
WHO-ARE
CALLED   BY-MY
NAME,   WILL
HUMBLE
THEMSELVES
AND-PRAY
AND-SEEK
MY-FACE
AND-TURN
FROM   THEIR
WICKED   WAYS,
THEN   WILL-
I   HEAR   FROM
HEAVEN
AND-WILL
FORGIVE   THEIR
SIN-AND   WILL
HEAL   THEIR
LAND.

Who was God talking to?

___ ___ ___ ___ ___ ___ ___
 1   2   3   4   5   6   7

Psalm 23:1, 6

Find and circle the words below in the puzzle grid. Words can be found going any direction up, down, diagonally, or backwards. Words connected with a hyphen, such as THE-LORD, are found as one word.

Spell out the missing words with the leftover letters. Can you fill in the missing words before you find them? After you complete the challenges, practice reciting the verse.

Bible Memory Verse

THE-LORD   IS-MY   SHEPHERD,
I-SHALL   NOT-BE   IN-WANT.
SURELY   GOODNESS   AND-
LOVE   __-__-__-__
FOLLOW   ME-ALL   THE-DAYS
OF-MY   LIFE,   AND-I   WILL
DWELL   IN-THE   HOUSE   OF-
THE   __-__-__-__   FOREVER.
__-__-__-__-__   23:1, 6

Word Search

```
W  L  L  A  H  S  I  I  O  L
E  S  U  O  H  Y  G  S  F  L
T  L  H  L  O  A  O  O  M  R
N  M  L  E  E  D  O  F  Y  Y
A  I  E  H  P  E  D  T  T  D
W  N  T  A  E  H  N  H  P  L
N  N  D  B  L  T  E  E  S  L
I  A  T  L  L  L  S  R  I  E
F  O  L  L  O  W  S  F  D  W
N  F  O  R  E  V  E  R  M  D
A  N  D  I  Y  L  E  R  U  S
```

Psalm 119:89, 90

Two words have been put together as one. Free the words by separating the letters.
The letters are found in the right order, but you decide which letter goes to which word.
Then unscramble the letters in the boxes to answer the question at the bottom of the page.

WYOORURD ☐ _ _ _   _ _ _ _ _ ,

LOORD _   _ _ _ _ ,

IETSERNAL _ _ _ _ _ _ _ ☐ ;

SITTANDS _ _   _ _ _ _

FINIRM _ _ _ ☐ _

HTEHAEVENS _ _ _   _ _ _ ☐ _ .

YFAOUIRTHFULNESS _ _ _ _ _   _ _ _ _ _ _ _ _ _ _

CTOHNRTOIUGHNHUES _ _ _ _ _ _ _ _   _ _ _ _ _ _ _

GALENLERATIONS _ _ _   _ _ ☐ _ _ _ _ _ _ _ _ ;

YEOSTABLISHEDU _ _ _   _ _ _ _ _ _ _ _ ☐

ETHARETH _ _ _   _ _ ☐ _ ☐ ,

IANTD _ _   _ ☐ _

PESNADLURMES _ _ _ _ _ _ .   _ _ _ _ ☐ 119:89, 90

The writer of this psalm loves God's Word.
What does he call God's law in verse 92?   ☐☐ ☐☐☐☐☐☐☐

Psalm 145:13

Strike out the extra Ps and Qs to reveal the last part of the Scripture verse. Caution! Some Ps or Qs may be needed to make the correct words.

```
P T P H E P L Q O P R Q Q D I Q S Q
P F Q A P I P Q T P H Q P F P U Q L
Q T O Q P A P L Q L P H Q I Q P S Q
P Q R Q O P M P P I P S Q E Q S Q Q
Q A Q N P P D L O Q V Q I P Q N P G
T P O W P Q A Q R D Q Q A Q L P P L
Q H P E H P P A P S Q M A P D Q Q E
P P S Q A P P L M P Q P 145:13 P Q P Q
```

Write the hidden verse here:

__ __ __   __ __ __ __   __ __

__ __ __ __ __ __ __ __ __

__ __   __ __ __ __ __ __ __

__ __ __ __ __ __ __ __ __

__ __ __ __ __ __ __ __ __ __

__ __ __ __ __ __ __ __ __

__ __   __ __ __   __ __ __ __ .

__ __ __ __ __ __   __ __ __ : __ __

Psalm 150:1, 2, 6

Decode each word by replacing each letter with one before or after it in the alphabet.

Replace A with Z or B, replace B with A or C, and so on.

When solved, the words spell out a Scripture verse.

The star ☆ shows an important word that has been left out. What is the word?

☆   S I D   K N Q E .   ☆   F P C   J O   G J T

T B O B U T Z S Z ;   ☆   I H L   J O   I H T

L J F G S X   G F B W D M R .   G H L

E P Q   I J T   B B U R   N G   O P X F Q ;

☆   G H L   G P Q   I H R   T V S Q B R T J M F

F S D B U M D R T .... K F S   D U D S Z S G J O H

S I B U   G Z T   A S F B U G   ☆   S G F

M P S C .   ☆   U G D   K N Q C .

Isaiah 12:2

When two letters go walking, only one does the talking. Discover the correct word by choosing only one letter from each pair to fill in the blank above the letters.

"

| SM | OU | RF | EI | LM | LY | | GQ | EO | VD | | OI | SZ | | FM | YL |

;

| TS | OA | LJ | BV | AE | BT | IU | OU | QN | | IA | | KW | EI | LW | LD |

| TF | FR | EU | SF | TP | | EA | NC | DV | | GN | OI | TX | | ZB | EI |

.   '

| AO | QF | RF | EA | EI | DN | | PT | KH | EA | | PL | AO | RX | DX |

'

| TP | QH | EO | | WL | OU | XR | BD | | IO | HS | | MW | GY |

| WS | TL | GR | UE | BN | GN | BT | LH | | IA | XN | DC | | MJ | YF |

;

| SG | OU | KN | ZG | | HG | EA | | HL | EA | MS | | WB | EO | PC | OU | MC | AE |

"

| MC | GY | | SM | EA | HL | VK | UA | HT | IU | AO | VN |

Matthew 10:2-4

Challenge 1: Unscramble the letters. All of the words are found in Matthew 10:2-4.

MNSAE   _ _ _ _ _

ELTEVW   _ _ _ _ _ _

SOSAPELT   _ _ _ _ _ _ _ _

ETEPR   _ _ _ _ _

DWENRA   _ _ _ _ _ _

ZEDEEEB   _ _ _ _ _ _

HNOJ   _ _ _ _

IIHPLP   _ _ _ _ _ _

HAMSTO   _ _ _ _ _ _

ATEWTHM   _ _ _ _ _ _ _

AMJES   _ _ _ _ _

EUSAHTDAD   _ _ _ _ _ _ _ _ _

NSMIO   _ _ _ _ _

JSADU   _ _ _ _ _

Challenge 2: Find and circle the unscrambled words.

```
T  H  P  I  L  I  H  P  E
M  M  A  T  T  H  E  W  T
I  S  P  S  W  T  I  H  N
G  A  O  W  E  E  A  P  J
O  S  S  R  E  D  L  O  A
N  S  T  S  D  R  H  V  M
O  A  L  A  E  N  D  T  E
M  D  E  M  B  M  L  N  S
I  U  S  O  E  E  A  I  A
S  J  S  H  Z  B  A  N  R
T  H  O  T  L  O  M  E  W
```

Challenge 3: One apostle is missing. Discover his name by spelling out the hidden phrase with the uncircled letters.

_ - _ - _   _ - _ - _ - _ - _ - _   _ - _ - _ - _ - _ - _

_ - _   _ - _ - _ - _ - _ - _ - _ - _ - _

Matthew 6:9-13

Use the word lists to fill in the blanks of Matthew 6:9-13.

3 letter word
ONE

4 letter words
ALSO
COME
DONE
GIVE
LEAD
WILL

5 letter words
BREAD
DAILY
DEBTS
EARTH
TODAY

6 letter words
FATHER
HEAVEN
HEAVEN

7 letter words
DEBTORS
DELIVER
KINGDOM

8 letter words
FORGIVEN
HALLOWED

10 letter word
TEMPTATION

"Our ▢▢▢▢▢▢ in ▢▢▢▢▢▢, ▢▢▢▢▢▢▢▢ be your name, your ▢▢▢▢▢▢▢ ▢▢▢▢, your ▢▢▢▢ be ▢▢▢▢ on ▢▢▢▢▢ as it is in ▢▢▢▢▢▢▢. ▢▢▢▢ us ▢▢▢▢▢ our ▢▢▢▢▢ ▢▢▢▢▢. Forgive us our ▢▢▢▢▢, as we ▢▢▢▢ have ▢▢▢▢▢▢▢▢ our ▢▢▢▢▢▢▢. And ▢▢▢▢ us not into ▢▢▢▢▢▢▢▢▢▢, but ▢▢▢▢▢▢▢ us from the evil ▢▢▢."

Matthew 22:37-39

Unscramble the letters and write them in the blanks. Match the numbered letters to the blanks at the bottom of the page for the phrase that completes the Scripture.

Jesus replied:

"EVLO _ _ _ _ TEH _ _ _ RODL _ _ _ _ ROYU _ _ _ _ _ ODG _ _ _
       18 3   4   1   8   5 2 19 15   6

TIHW _ _ _ _ LAL _ _ _ your EARTH _ _ _ _ _ and with all your
      11 13   16 23   10

ULOS _ _ _ _ and with all your NIMD _ _ _ _ . This is the RITSF _ _ _ _ _
      14 7   9   24   20 21

and TEGRAEST _ _ _ _ _ _ _ _ commandment. And the second is like it:
             12 22   17

_ _ _ _   _ _ _ _   _ _ _ _ _ B _ _
1 2 3 4   5 6 7 8   9 10 11 12 13 14 15

                                        "
_ _   _ _ _ _ _ _ _ _
16 17   5 18 19 20 21 22 23 24

Matthew 28:19, 20

Find the **BOLDFACE** words in the puzzle grid and circle them.
The uncircled letters in the puzzle grid spell out the hidden phrase.

THEREFORE go and **MAKE DISCIPLES** of all **NATIONS**, **BAPTIZING THEM** in the **NAME** of the **FATHER** and of the Son and of the **HOLY SPIRIT**, and **TEACHING** them to **OBEY EVERYTHING** I **HAVE COMMANDED** you. And **SURELY** I am **WITH** you **ALWAYS**, to the **VERY** end of the age."

Matthew 28:19, 20

```
J A S E S U T T S E T
Y L E R U S H T V E L
E W L L S E E E H D I
B A P S M K R A R E D
O Y I I A Y E C E D S
S S C M T C F H H N I
P P S H S N O I T A N
L W I T H L R N A M E
E N D R Y S E G F M V
G N I Z I T P A B O A
W H A T T T O D O C H
```

Hidden Phrase: __ -- __ -- __ -- __ -- __   __ -- __ -- __ -- __ -- __   __ -- __ -- __

__ -- __ -- __ -- __ -- __ -- __ -- __   __ -- __ -- __ -- __   __ -- __   __ -- __

Romans 1:16

Discover the hidden verse! In the message below, some of the letters are filled in for you. Use them to figure out the code, and then solve the puzzle. Memorize this great verse about the power of God!

```
__   ___   ____   __   _ S ____ E __   __   __ E   G _ S _ E _,
18   10 22  23 24 3  10 2 17 10 22 14 13  24 15  3 17 14  16 24 2 25 14 21

__ E ____ S E   __   _ S   _ E   ____ E _   __   _ G
11 14 12 10 4 2 14  18 3  18 2  3 17 14  25 24 6 14 1  24 15  16 24 13

____   __ E S _____   __   E _ E ____ E
15 24 1  3 17 14  2 10 21 5 10 3 18 24 23  24 15  14 5 14 1 8 24 23 14

___   __ E __ E _ E S:   ____ S _   ___   ___   __ E _,
6 17 24  11 14 21 18 14 5 14 2  15 18 1 2 3  15 24 1  3 17 14  19 14 6

__ E __   ___   __ E   G E ____ E
3 17 14 23  15 24 1  3 17 14  16 14 23 3 18 21 14
```

	14		16						2																
A	B	C	D	E	F	G	H	I	J	K	L	M	N	O	P	Q	R	S	T	U	V	W	X	Y	Z

Help the letters into their boxes. Raise the letters to their correct boxes directly above them to spell out the hidden message. The message reads from left to right and then down. Boxes with punctuation have no letters.

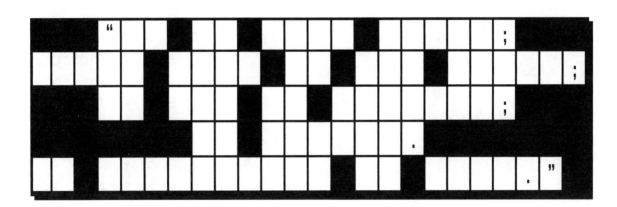

```
S O A N E E M O T H Y F U R N G U L G V E T H
D T   B B E R I E M I N G O I N E A F D I
    E D   F E R   O I R C T U R A R E
    V     B N   S O N   O G     O A
    Y     N     T     H
```

Galatians 5:22-25

Find and circle the words from Galatians 5:24 in the puzzle grid.
Use the uncircled letters to fill in the blanks below.

THOSE WHO BELONG
TO CHRIST JESUS HAVE
CRUCIFIED THE SINFUL
NATURE WITH ITS
PASSIONS AND DESIRES.

```
E  S  O  H  T  S  D  L  L  B
I  V  E  L  U  E  E  U  H  E
I  T  U  S  S  S  F  A  D  L
T  K  E  I  E  N  V  E  E  O
S  J  R  P  I  E  I  N  I  N
S  E  T  S  E  P  W  T  F  G
S  H  T  I  W  W  H  O  I  I
T  S  I  R  H  C  T  H  C  T
H  H  E  R  U  T  A  N  U  E
S  P  E  I  A  N  D  R  R  I
P  A  S  S  I  O  N  S  C  T
```

Since we ☐☐☐☐ by the Spirit,

☐☐☐ ☐☐ ☐☐☐☐ ☐☐☐ ☐☐☐☐☐

☐☐☐☐ ☐☐☐ ☐☐☐☐☐☐☐.

Galatians 5:25

Hebrews 11:1, 6

Bible
Memory

Find and circle the words in the puzzle grid. Words can be found going
any direction up, down, diagonally, or backwards. Words connected
with a hyphen, such as NOW-FAITH, are found as one word.

Spell out the missing words with the leftover letters. Can you fill in the missing words
before you find them? After you complete the challenges, practice reciting the verse.

Memory Verse

NOW-FAITH   IS-BEING   SURE-
OF   WHAT-WE   HOPE   FOR-
AND   CERTAIN   OF-WHAT
WE-DO   NOT-SEE .

_-_-_   _-_-_-_-_-_
_-_-_-_-_   IT-IS

_-_-_-_-_-_-_-_
TO-PLEASE   GOD-BECAUSE
ANYONE   WHO-COMES   TO-
HIM   MUST   BELIEVE   THAT-
HE   EXISTS   AND-THAT   HE-
REWARDS   THOSE-WHO
EARNESTLY   SEEK-HIM .

_-_-_-_-_-_-_ 11:1, 6.

Word Search

```
E V E I L E B A N D W I
A S E M O C O H W T S H
R G U E A N D T H A T O
N N U A S T F E O N S A
E I N I C T R F H Y I E
S E T O S E O H W O X P
T B S U W E B N E N E O
L S M A R F E D S E F H
Y I R U E W A K O W I F
M D S O T L M I H G P O
S I D A I O P A T I S R
S E H T A H T O I H M A
W W I O B C E R T A I N
L S E H T E B R E W S D
```

BIBLE PUZ*LES for KIDS Ages 8–10   131

2 Peter 3:18

Write the letter tiles in the correct order in the boxes below to reveal the Bible Memory verse.

JESU	W IN	HIM	RIST	CE A	OREV	AND
GLOR	. TO	ER!	ER 3	SAV	OW A	NOWL
AMEN	: 18	LORD	." 2	"BUT	EDGE	GRO
Y BO	BE	S CH	OUR	TH N	IOR	GRA
ND F	THE	ND K	OF	PET		

Revelation 22:20

Raise the letters to the correct boxes directly above them to spell out the hidden message. The message reads from left to right and then down. Boxes with punctuation have no letters. The first letter of some words has not fallen.

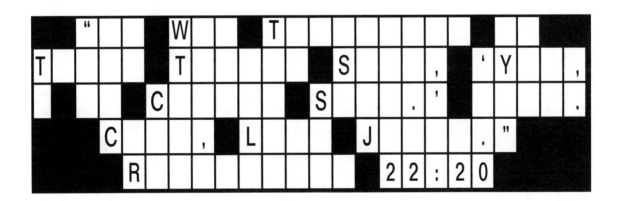

```
I H E M E E E H O N G E S N A Y S E S A T E N
A H O M V E L A T R D T I E I U S   M O S
S E   O M I N O S O O N S           E
    H I   G I       F
```

Answers to Puzzles

Page 9
ACROSS: 1. sixth; 4. fifth;
5. rested; 7. fourth. DOWN:
2. third; 3. first; 6. second

Page 10
1. Adam and Eve; 2. good;
3. figs; 4. trees; 5. serpent;
6. wisdom; 7. fruit; 8. evil

Page 11
Noah found favor in the eyes of
the Lord. (Genesis 6:8)

Page 12
ACROSS: 1. language; 2. plain;
3. no; 4. stone; 5. Shinar;
6. Lord. DOWN: 1. Babylonia;
2. heavens; 3. name; 4. tower;
5. brick

Page 13

Page 14
1. Isaac—He laughs; 2. Moses—
Drawn out; 3. Adam—Man;
4. Sarah—Princess;
5. Eve—Life

Page 15
Here I am! (see Genesis 22:1)

Page 16
Birthright: A double share of the
inheritance and leadership of the
clan.

Page 17
Dinah (Genesis 30:21)

Page 18
6 (letter e), 2 (letter s), 1 (letter o),
5 (letter e), 3 (letter o), 4 (letter n)

Page 19
A. 3; B. 6; C. 1; D. 4; E. 2; F. 5

Page 20

Page 21

Page 22
1. lamb; 2. blood; 3. herbs;
4. bread; 5. none; 6. cloak;
7. sandals

Page 23

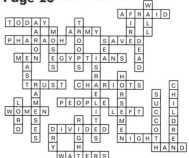

Page 24
"The most important one",
answered Jesus, "is this: . . . 'Love
the Lord your God with all your
heart and with all your soul and
with all your mind and with all
your strength.'" (Mark 12:29, 30)

Page 25
"No one will be able to stand up
against you all the days of your
life. As I was with Moses, so I will
be with you; I will never leave
you nor forsake you."
(Joshua 1:5)

Page 26
"He did this so that all the peoples
of the earth might know that the
hand of the Lord is powerful and
so that you might always fear the
Lord your God." (Joshua 4:24)

Answers to Puzzles

Page 27

When the trumpets sounded, the people shouted, . . . when the people gave a loud shout, the wall collapsed; so every man charged straight in, and they took the city. (Joshua 6:20)

Page 28

Deborah, a prophetess, the wife of Lappidoth, was leading Israel at that time. She held court under the palm of Deborah . . . and the Israelites came to her to have their disputes decided. (Judges 4:4, 5)

Page 29

The Lord confused the enemy soldiers.

Page 30

Now in earlier times in Israel, for the redemption and transfer of property to become final, one party took off his sandal and gave it to the other. This was the method of legalizing transactions in Israel. (Ruth 4:7)

Page 31

Then Samuel took a flask of oil and poured it on Saul's head and kissed him, saying, "Has not the Lord anointed you leader over his inheritance?" (1 Samuel 10:1)

Page 32

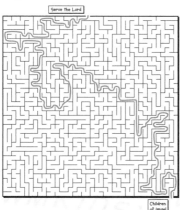

Page 33

"My father made your yoke heavy; I will make it even heavier. My father scourged you with whips; I will scourge you with scorpions." (1 Kings 12:14)

Page 34

"And He will give Israel up because of the sins Jeroboam has committed and has caused Israel to commit." (1 Kings 14:16)

Page 35

The ravens brought him bread and meat in the morning and bread and meat in the evening, and he drank from the brook. (1 Kings 17:6)

Page 36

He went in, shut the door on the two of them and prayed to the Lord. Then he got on the bed and lay upon the boy, mouth to mouth, eyes to eyes, hands to hands. As he stretched himself out upon him, the boy's body grew warm. (2 Kings 4:33, 34)

Page 37

Trust in the Lord with all your heart and lean not on your own understanding; in all your ways acknowledge him, and he will make your paths straight. (Proverbs 3:5, 6)

Page 38

All the people and officials gladly brought their offerings and dropped them in the chest until it was full.

Page 39

"Grant me my life." "Spare my people."

Page 40

The Lord is my shepherd, I shall not be in want. He makes me lie down in green pastures, he leads me beside quiet waters, he restores my soul. (Psalm 23:1-3)

Page 41

Shout with joy to God, all the earth! Sing the glory of his name; make his praise glorious! (Psalm 66:1, 2)

Page 42

He set the earth on its foundations; it can never be moved. (Psalm 104:5)

Page 43

I have hidden your word in my heart that I might not sin against you. (Psalm 119:11)

Answers to Puzzles

Page 44
"The virgin will be with child and will give birth to a son." (Isaiah 7:14)

Page 45
"If...I announce that a nation or kingdom is to be...destroyed, and if that nation...repents of its evil, then I will relent and not inflict on it the disaster I had planned." (Jeremiah 18:7, 8)

Page 46
"For I know the plans I have for you," declares the Lord, "plans to prosper you and not to harm you, plans to give you hope and a future." (Jeremiah 29:11)

Page 47
Vegetables and water to drink.

Page 48
Daniel was found innocent in God's sight, nor had he ever done any wrong before King Darius. (Daniel 6:22)

Page 49
The king of Nineveh put on sack-cloth and declared that no one should eat or drink, but everyone should call on the Lord and give up their evil ways.

Page 51
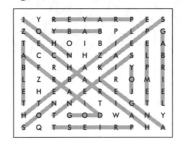

Page 52
1. mouse; 2. sheep; 3. dove; 4. horse; 5. chicken; 6. cow

Page 53
1. angel; 2. Jesus; 3. Jerusalem; 4. pigeons; 5. Simeon; 6. Anna; 7. Nazareth

Page 54
1. virtue; 2. prayer; 3. suffering

Page 55
"Didn't you know I had to be in my Father's house?" (Luke 2:49)

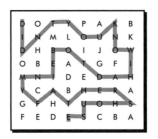

Page 56
It is written, "Worship the Lord your God and serve Him only." "Do not put the Lord your God to the test." (Luke 4:8, 12)

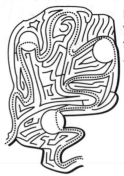

Page 57

Page 58

Page 59

Page 60

Leper, sick, crippled, dead, paralyzed, deaf, mute, blind, insane, bleeding

Page 61

Page 62

Verse 3-C or E; 4-A; 5-B; 6-G; 7-I; 8-H; 9-F; 10-C or E; 11, 12-D

Page 63

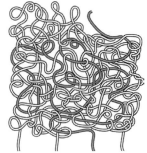

Let Us Pray

Page 64

Sand, rain, stand, rock, long, say, do, Lord, you

Page 65

TRUST

Page 66

"But the seed on good soil stands for those with a noble and good heart, who hear the word, retain it, and by persevering produce a crop." (Luke 8:15)

Page 67

Then he got up and rebuked the winds and the waves, and it was completely calm. (Matthew 8:26)

Page 68

"Go home to your family and tell them how much the Lord has done for you, and how he has had mercy on you." (Mark 5:19)

Page 69

So they gathered them and filled twelve baskets with the pieces of the five barley loaves left over by those who had eaten. (John 6:13)

Page 70

Simon Peter answered, "You are the Christ, the Son of the living God." (Matthew 16:16)

Page 71

Lightning lights up the sky, while Jesus lights up our hearts. Jesus is the light that guides us to our heavenly home.

Page 72

"Forgive your brother from your heart." (Matthew 18:35)

Page 73

"So I say to you: Ask and it will be given to you; seek and you will find, knock and the door will be opened to you." (Luke 11:9)

Page 74

"I tell you that in the same way there will be more rejoicing in heaven over one sinner who repents than over ninety-nine righteous persons who do not need to repent." (Luke 15:7)

Page 75

LAZARUS COME OUT

Page 76

"Go," said Jesus, "your faith has healed you." Immediately he received his sight and followed Jesus along the road. (Mark 10:52)

Page 77

Jesus replied: "'Love the Lord your God with all your heart and with all your soul and with all your mind.' This is the first and greatest commandment." (Matthew 22:37, 38)

Page 78

"Therefore keep watch, because you do not know the day or the hour." (Matthew 25:13)

Page 79

Each one should use whatever gift he has received to serve others, faithfully administering God's grace in its various forms. (1 Peter 4:10)

Page 80

The bread, which represents His body. The cup, which represents His blood.

Answers to Puzzles

Page 81

After Jesus was arrested and taken away, He was led to the palace where the soldiers mocked Him. They dressed Him in a purple robe and placed a crown of twisted thorns on His head. They called Him the King of the Jews, struck Him on the head with a staff, then spit on Him. When they finished, they put His clothes back on Him and led Him away to be crucified.

Page 82

"He has risen from the dead and is going ahead of you into Galilee. There you will see him." (Matthew 28:7)

Page 83

"Because you have seen me, you have believed; blessed are those who have not seen and yet have believed." (John 20:29)

Page 84

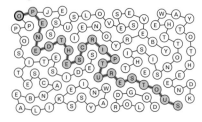

"Were not our hearts burning within us while he talked with us on the road and opened the Scriptures to us?" (Luke 24:32)

Page 85

"Surely I am with you always, to the very end of the age." (Matthew 28:20)

Page 86

"Repent and be baptized." (Acts 2:38)

Page 87

"Silver or gold I do not have, but what I have I give you. In the name of Jesus Christ of Nazareth, walk." (Acts 3:6)

Page 88

"Salvation is found in no one else, for there is no other name under heaven given to men by which we must be saved." (Acts 4:12)

Page 89

"I see heaven open and the Son of Man standing at the right hand of God." (Acts 7:56)

Page 90

"Look, here is water. Why shouldn't I be baptized?" (Acts 8:36)

Page 91

"Go! This man is my chosen instrument." (Acts 9:15)

Page 92

Peter knelt, prayed, and told Dorcas to get up and she did.

Page 93

Peter said: "I now realize how true it is that God does not show favoritism but accepts men from every nation who fear Him and do what is right." (Acts 10:34, 35)

Page 94

"Now I know without a doubt that the Lord sent his angel and rescued me from Herod's clutches." (Acts 12:11)

Page 95

"Men, why are you doing this? We too are only men, human like you." (Acts 14:15)

Page 96

The Lord opened her heart to respond to Paul's message. . . . She and the members of her household were baptized. (Acts 16:14, 15)

Page 97

1. teeth; 2. jail; 3. television; 4. hand; 5. south; 6. shadow; 7. dream; 8. rust; 9. scream; 10. reel. As a result the jailor and his entire household were saved.

Page 98

Eutychus

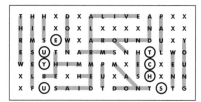

Page 99

Ananias; Paul; Sadducees; commander; the Lord; the Jews; Paul's nephew; centurion. Pharisee (Acts 23:6)

Page 100

Page 101
The gift of God is eternal life in Christ Jesus our Lord.

Page 102
1. false; 2. true; 3. false; 4. false; 5. true; 6. true. Therefore, as we have opportunity, let us do good to all people, especially to those who belong to the family of believers. (Galations 6:10)

Page 103
Love, joy, peace, patience, kindness, goodness, faithfulness, gentleness, self-control.

Page 104
1. truth (belt); 2. readiness that comes from the gospel of peace (feet); 3. salvation (helmet); 4. Word of God (sword); 5. righteousness (breastplate); 6. faith (shield)

Page 105
Across—2. children; 3. everything; 5. stand. Down—1. shine; 4. God; 6. always

Page 106
Be joyful always; pray continually; give thanks in all circumstances, for this is God's will for you in Christ Jesus. (1 Thessalonians 5:16-18)

Page 107
Show true humility; set them an example; do whatever is good; be obedient; be self-controlled; be peaceable; and considerate; hope of eternal life; show integrity. Have faith.

Page 108
Come near to God and he will come near to you. (James 4:8)

Page 109
Dear friends, let us love one another (v. 7); This is love: not that we loved God, but that he loved us (v. 10); Since God so loved us, we also ought to love one another (v. 11); Whoever lives in love lives in God, and God in him (v. 16); We love because he first loved us (v. 19); Whoever loves God must also love his brother (v. 21).

Page 110

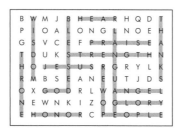

Page 111
"I am the Alpha and the Omega." "I am coming soon." "I will give to everyone according to what he has done." "I am the . . . bright Morning Star." Come, Lord Jesus.

Page 112
Power, great, marvelous, righteous, salvation, true, holy, king, almighty. Praise him.

Page 113
In the beginning God created the heavens and the earth. (Genesis 1:1)

Page 114
"Abraham will surely become a great and powerful nation, and all nations on earth will be blessed through him." (Genesis 18:18)

Page 115
Who, is, like, in, Exodus

Page 116
Love the Lord your God with all your heart and with all your soul and with all your strength. (Deuteronomy 6:5) Upon your hearts (v. 6).

Page 117
Courageous, do, not, be, discouraged

Page 118
Solomon

Page 119
will, Lord, Psalm

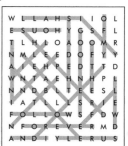

Answers to Puzzles

Page 120
Your word, O Lord, is eternal; it stands firm in the heavens. Your faithfulness continues through all generations; you established the earth, and it endures. Psalm 119:89, 90; my delight.

Page 121
The Lord is faithful to all his promises and loving toward all he has made. Psalm 145:13

Page 122
The star word is *praise*. Praise the Lord. Praise God in his sanctuary; praise him in his mighty heavens. Praise him for his acts of power; praise him for his surpassing greatness. . . . Let everything that has breath praise the Lord. Praise the Lord.

Page 123
"Surely God is my salvation; I will trust and not be afraid. The Lord, the Lord, is my strength and my song; he has become my salvation." (Isaiah 12:2)

Page 124
The missing apostle is Bartholomew.

Page 125
"Our Father in heaven, hallowed be your name, your kingdom come, your will be done on earth as it is in heaven. Give us today our daily bread. Forgive us our debts, as we also have forgiven our debtors. And lead us not into temptation, but deliver us from the evil one." (Matthew 6:9-13)

Page 126
Jesus replied: "Love the Lord your God with all your heart and with all your soul and with all your mind. This is the first and greatest commandment. And the second is like it: Love your neighbor as yourself." (Matthew 22:37-39)

Page 127
Jesus tells his disciples what to do

Page 128
I am not ashamed of the gospel, because it is the power of God for the salvation of everyone who believes: first for the Jew, then for the Gentile. (Romans 1:16)

Page 129

Page 130
Since we live by the Spirit, let us keep in step with the Spirit. (Galatians 5:25)

Page 131
And, without, faith, impossible, Hebrews

Page 132
"But grow in the grace and knowledge of our Lord and Savior Jesus Christ. To him be glory both now and forever! Amen." (2 Peter 3:18)

Page 133
"He who testifies to these things says, 'Yes, I am coming soon.' Amen. Come, Lord Jesus." (Revelation 22:20)

Scope & Sequence

HeartShaper™ Middle Elementary Scope & Sequence

HeartShaper® Middle Elementary

Bible Memory Puzzles

Middle Elementary Bible Memory Puzzles

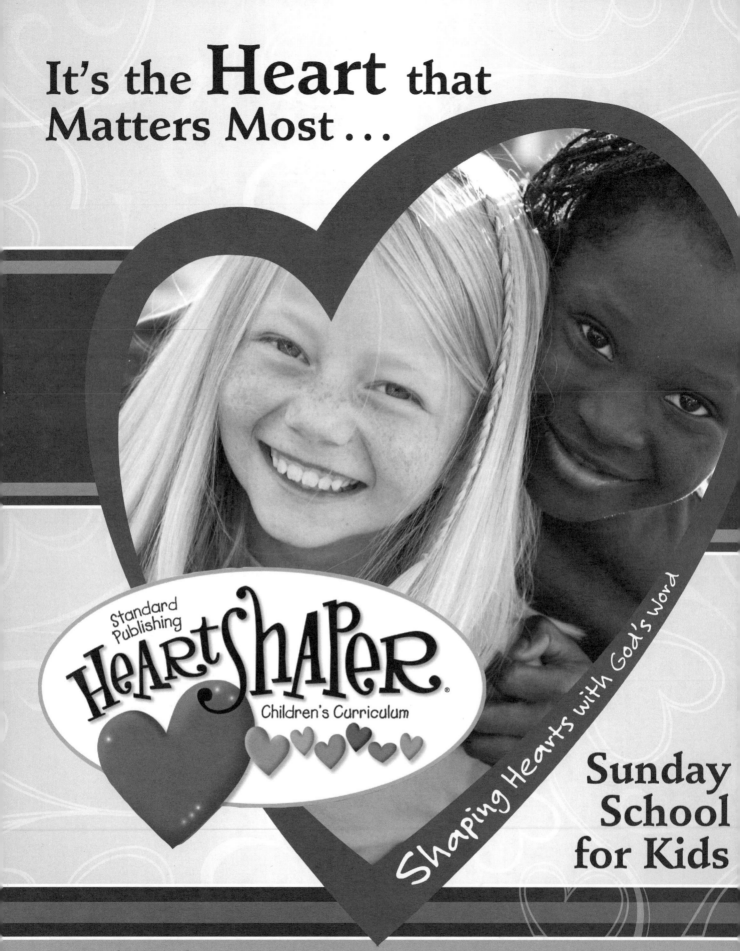

It's the **Heart** that Matters Most...

HeARtSHAPeR
Standard Publishing
Children's Curriculum

Shaping Hearts with God's Word

Sunday School for Kids

www.heartshaper.com
For more information call
1-800-543-1353

Standard
PUBLISHING
www.standardpub.com